" *OUTSTANDING BOOK!* Personality at Work *delivers on its promise—an amazing job of turning theory into concrete action plans.* "

Keith B. Grant, Ph.D.
Internal Consultant
General Motors

" *COMPREHENSIVE AND STATE-OF-THE-ART RESEARCH. Should be read by anyone who is dedicated to helping people and organizations get the best from individual talents. Shows how to capitalize on strengths and manage weaknesses instead of swimming upstream.* "

Nico Smid, Ph.D.
Senior Consultant, PiMedia
Netherlands

" *A VALUABLE RESOURCE that adds to the toolkit of any trainer working in the field of personality.* "

Bridget Seddon
Business Development Director, The PACT Group
United Kingdom

" *REAL WORLD—REAL BUSINESS APPLICATIONS. Helps people understand and apply the concepts to everyday performance improvement.* "

Gary L. Selden, Ed.D.
Assistant Professor, Coles College of Business
Kennesaw State University

" *EXTREMELY WELL WRITTEN. Anyone interested in personality assessment and how it impacts performance in the workplace will find* Personality at Work *very useful.* "

John H. (Jack) Zenger
Vice Chairman
Provant, Inc.

*" **BASED ON SOUND SCIENTIFIC RESEARCH,** it shows how to develop and optimize the human dimension of organizations. Helps us understand why individuals and groups behave the way they do and how to best develop, support, and compensate performance-critical behaviors. "*

Shakeel Pal
Senior HR Generalist
Citibank N.A., Pakistan

*" **THIS BOOK HAS THE ABILITY TO CHANGE ONE'S LIFE.** With readable language, realistic examples, and practical usage, it helps us understand that our differences are our strengths—and it greatly enhances the performance of individuals and teams. "*

Jennifer P. Davis
President & CEO
JP Davis & Associates, Inc.

*" **MAKES COMPLICATED MATERIAL SEEM EASY.** It will reveal many new understandings about yourself and others. "*

Terry Armstrong, Ph.D.
Scholar-in-Residence
Emerson College

*" **OUTSTANDING!** Ties personality to performance with a complete explanation of the Big Five personality model. Full of real-life examples. "*

Angie Hardison
Manager of Organizational Development
SCANA

THE
Owner's Manual FOR
Personality
AT Work

**HOW THE
BIG FIVE PERSONALITY TRAITS
AFFECT
PERFORMANCE, COMMUNICATION, TEAMWORK,
LEADERSHIP, AND SALES**

Pierce J. Howard, Ph.D.
Jane Mitchell Howard, M.B.A.

**Bard
Press**

AUSTIN ★ ATLANTA

The Owner's Manual for Personality at Work
How the Big Five Personality Traits Affect Performance,
Communication, Teamwork, Leadership, and Sales

Printed in the United States of America

Bard Press
An imprint of Longstreet Press
2140 Newmarket Parkway, Suite 122
Marietta, GA 30067
Phone 770-980-1488   Fax 770-859-9894
www.bardpress.com

ISBN 1-885167-45-8 (pbk)

Library of Congress Cataloging-in-Publication Data

Howard, Pierce J.
   The owner's manual for personality at work : how the big five personality traits affect performance, communication, teamwork, leadership, and sales / Pierce J. Howard, Jane Mitchell Howard.
     p. cm.
   Includes bibliographical references and index.
   ISBN 1-885167-45-8 (pbk)
     1. Personality and occupation.   2. Prediction of occupational success.   3. Employees—Psychological testing.   4. Work—Psychological aspects.   5. Personality tests.
   I. Howard, Jane Mitchell, 1952–   II. Title.
   BF698.9.O3 H69 2000
   155.2'3—dc21   00-046754

        Printed in Canada
The authors may be contacted through
        *Cent*ACS—the Center for Applied Cognitive Studies
        1100 Harding Place
        Charlotte, NC 28204
        704-331-0926 phone
        704-331-9408 fax
        info@centacs.com or www.centacs.com

A BARD PRESS BOOK
Copyediting: Helen Hyams
Proofreading: Helen Hyams, Deborah Costenbader, Luke Torn
Index: Linda Webster
Text and Cover Design: Suzanne Pustejovsky
Composition: Round Rock Graphics

First printing: December 2000

Dedication

As partners in life and work, the two of us have many commonalities—from personality and values, to hobbies and interests, to family and spiritual growth environments. One unique environmental attribute we share is that we both grew up as if we were only children, even though we have always had siblings. This is possible because we were both "mistakes" for our parents: we were never intended to be in this world. When Pierce arrived, his parents already had three daughters and three sons who were all ages seventeen and older. When Jane was born, her two sisters were fourteen and sixteen.

As a result of all these extra parent-like siblings and our more experienced parents, we feel that our childhoods and teenage years were especially joyful and gave us rich and varied life experiences that have benefited us throughout our lives and careers. We would like to express our thanks for the love and care our parents and siblings gave us by dedicating this book to them.

Our parents:

Alonza DeWitt Mitchell

Edith Dennis Mitchell

Curtis William Howard, Jr.

Eleanor Johnson Howard

Our siblings:

Carolyn Mitchell Barber

Janelle Mitchell Williams

Virginia Howard McGahey

Nancy Howard Sitterson

Eleanor Howard Cummings

Curtis William Howard III

Lee Johnson Howard

Alexander Blucher Howard

We would also like to dedicate this book to our two wonderful daughters, Allegra Howard Hinson and Hilary Ren Howard, and our son-in-law, William Carl Hinson IV, who in their adulthood have also become our best friends, especially as we and they have better understood personalities in the home as well as the workplace.

Table of Contents

Acknowledgments

Acknowledgment pages should perhaps increase in volume from a barely detectable rumble to ear-piercing thunder and lightning. Please do not, however, interpret the order of these names as an indication of the degree of significance they have played in the creation of this book. Each has been a necessary voice in the composition that is now a book:

—**Our customers,** without whom we never would have gone down the path of human resource consulting.

—**Our investors,** without whom we never would have been able to launch our business.

—**Our global Big Five consulting network,** without whom we never would have been able to let go of our old consulting work in order to focus on Big Five research and dissemination.

—**Our international affiliates,** without whom our focus would be provincial to the point of naïveté.

—**Our manuscript readers,** Mark Ardis, Stephen Brock, Caryn Colgan, Joachim de Posada, Carolyn Nash Edwards, Richard Grant, Vicki Halsey, Michael Herbert, Susan Hewitt, Marsha Jackson, Gary John, Shirley Lim, Teresa Oliszewicz, Gerry Singleton, and Jack Zenger, without whom our point of view would have been far more inward than outward.

—**Our team at _Cent_ACS,** Rita Burke, Carol Coscia, Ted Hessberg, and Jo Washington, without whom we would have had to put in forty-eight-hour days in order to finish on schedule.

—**Our university colleagues and interns,** from Davidson College, Pfeiffer University at Charlotte, and the University of North Carolina at Charlotte, without whom it would have taken another decade to collect and analyze normative and validity data for the new Workplace Big Five ProFile.

—**Bob Smith and Serje Seminoff** of Psychological Assessment Resources, Tampa, Florida, publisher of the NEO tests, without whose encouragement we would never have focused exclusively on the Five-Factor Model.

—**Wayne Clark,** whose visual artistry has created our recognizable and highly praised image in the marketplace.

—**Chip Bell,** without whose encouragement and introduction to Ray Bard we never would have dared to start a book.

—**Ray Bard,** our publisher, whose flexibility, vision, companionship, and resourcefulness have made authorship a deeply pleasurable chapter in our professional lives.

—**Cathy Lewis,** our publicist, who has an extraordinary knack for opening doors to both Main Street and backwater U.S.A.

—**Suzanne Pustejovsky,** a rare book designer who has transformed four hundred pages of double-spaced Courier (*bo*-ring!) into this visually appealing and reader-friendly volume.

—**Helen Hyams,** editor extraordinaire, who combines the rarely united qualities of thoroughgoing criticality and enthusiastic support.

—**To each other,** for patience, solace, creativity, and fun in the face of long hours, hurried meals, and seemingly unending revisions.

Thanks, team!

Pierce and Jane
September 28, 2000
Charlotte, North Carolina

The
Authors

Pierce J. Howard, Ph.D., is a general partner and director of research for *Cent*ACS, the Center for Applied Cognitive Studies in Charlotte, North Carolina. Since starting the company in 1986 with his partner and wife, Jane, Pierce has specialized in team building, assessment, and the most current research in cognitive science, especially regarding the Five-Factor Model of personality. He now manages *Cent*ACS' research division, compiling data from ongoing research projects on the Five-Factor Model, developing software applications, and continuing to develop and teach the Big Five certification program with Jane.

Pierce received his Ph.D. degree in education with a special interest in curriculum and research in 1972 from the University of North Carolina at Chapel Hill. For the last twenty-five years, he has been an organizational psychologist. Since 1996, he has taught both organization behavior and problem solving for managers for the M.B.A. program at Pfeiffer University in Charlotte. He also teaches in the University of North Carolina–Charlotte certificate program in organization development.

Pierce is the author of *The Owner's Manual for the Brain: Everyday Applications from Mind-Brain Research*. He and his book were featured on "The Oprah Winfrey Show" in May 1997. He and Jane have coauthored workbooks, manuals, and articles on the Five-Factor Model and are frequently presenters at regional, national, and international conferences. Pierce's professional affiliations include the American Psychological Association, International Society for the Study of Individual Differences, North Carolina Psychological Association, American Society for Training and Development, and the Carolinas Organization Development Network.

Jane Mitchell Howard, M.B.A., is a general partner and the managing director of *Cent*ACS, where she oversees the promotion, marketing, sales, operations, information technology, finance, and programmatic aspects of the company. Since 1991, Jane has worked with clients in using the Five-Factor Model of personality, developed Big Five materials, conducted executive coaching, led team-building retreats and sessions with the Big Five, integrated the Big Five into training programs, and, with Pierce, developed and continues to teach the Big Five certification program for consultants and trainers. She also manages the international affiliate network that *Cent*ACS has developed.

Jane received her M.B.A. degree with a concentration in organization behavior in 1987 from the Babcock Graduate School of Management at Wake Forest University. A member of the Charlotte Area Chapter of the American Society for Training and Development since 1982, Jane was president of the chapter in 1989 and was National ASTD's 1990 Regional Director for Region 4. In 1993, she received the chapter's annual Excellence in Service to the Community Award, and in 1995, she received the National ASTD's Women's Network Professional Development Leadership Award. Jane also serves on the Steering Committee for the Carolinas Organization Development Network. She has been active on the Educational Services Committee for the Charlotte Chamber of Commerce and on the Volunteer Personnel Committee of the Carolinas Region of the American Red Cross, and has been president of the Carolinas Organization Development Interest Group.

Like Pierce, Jane teaches in the University of North Carolina–Charlotte certificate program in organization development, and they have both presented sessions for conferences in the United States, Europe, Central America, and Asia. Together, the Howards wrote the first article about the Big Five that was ever published in a trade journal. Their article, "Buddy, Can You Paradigm?" was published in the September 1995 issue of *Training and Development*.

Introduction

The Owner's Manual for Using This Book

Take a few minutes with us to consider how to get the most benefit from this book. The book is not exclusively either an academic textbook or a how-to manual; however, it is oriented more toward application than toward theory. Although we will pay appropriate homage to the researchers, our emphasis will be on applying their knowledge to the workplace. Thus, this introduction is really an "Owner's Manual" for the "Owner's Manual." In it we will give you several pointers that will help you to focus effectively on this book as a professional resource.

" Time spent in planning is saved in execution. "

—Management adage

How Did You Come to This Book?

Perhaps you were browsing at your favorite bookstore, or in a bookstore new to you, far from home, on vacation or on a business trip, and you came upon this book in the business or psychology section. You may have absolutely no background in studying personality models or dynamics, you may have an extensive background, or you may fall somewhere in between.

If you are a shopper who has had no introduction to the Big Five personality model and you find that you'd like more personalized assistance than this book can provide, we suggest that you visit our website at www.centacs.com. There you'll find two particularly helpful kinds of resources: first, a guide to additional resources—printed materials, websites, training opportunities, and so forth—and second, a listing of affiliate companies and consultants from around the world who have been trained in the Big Five personality model and ways to use it for professional growth, and who would be delighted to work with you and your organization. A logical next step for you would be to take a Big Five questionnaire. Knowing your scores will increase your depth of understanding of the material in this book.

If you are someone who has received brief feedback in a training class, coaching session, career planning class, team retreat, or some similar format and who desires to go into the model more deeply, this book will serve to cement new learnings from these training and development activities by providing you with a "take-home" tool to use in reviewing them and exploring them in greater depth. Why go into more depth? Because we know (Detterman and Sternberg, 1993) that on average, 90 percent of every training and development dollar is wasted because of a failure to transfer the learning back to the job. In addition to follow-up, however, this book can also be used as preparation for receiving feedback. Reading it *before* getting feedback from a Big Five test will make the feedback that much more meaningful.

Or perhaps you have attended a training, team-building, coaching, or other kind of session in which the session leader used a Big Five questionnaire and personal report with you, and the session leader either gave you this book or recommended that you get a copy for follow-up. In this case, you already have your scores. Keep them handy as you read this book.

Perhaps you are a trainer or other human resource professional who knows the Big Five in depth already. We think you'll find that this book is a helpful refresher course. Or perhaps you've learned about the Big Five from a source other than our organization. In that case, we hope you'll find our perspective an enriching one for your professional practice.

Perhaps you are a regular citizen who has discovered this book by chance. If so, we hope you benefit from reading our work. Let us know if you'd like ideas for ways to follow up.

Or perhaps an associate has given or loaned you this book. In that case, find out if she or he can arrange for you to complete a Big Five questionnaire. You'll find your reading much more meaningful if you do so.

How to Read This Book More Selectively

Certainly we encourage you to read this book from cover to cover! However, we know the time crunch most of you face. If you want a more streamlined approach, see if one of these approaches fits better for you:

Everyone: Read Chapters One through Seven.

Managers: Focus on Chapters Eight, Twelve, and Fourteen through Seventeen.

Team members: Focus on Chapters Nine, Eleven, and Twelve.

Salespeople: Focus on Chapters Nine and Eleven.

Educators, including trainers, teachers, and instructional designers: Focus on Part Three (Chapters Fourteen through Seventeen), plus any specific chapters in Part Two that apply to your special area of interest or responsibility.

People with a "life after work": Focus on Chapter Eighteen.

People who are in conflict with others: Focus on Chapters Nine, Eleven, and Fourteen.

People in career transition: Focus on Chapters Ten, Fourteen, Fifteen, and Sixteen.

Team leaders: Focus on Chapters Eight, Eleven, and Twelve.

People with hiring and staffing responsibility: Focus on Chapters Eight through Ten and Thirteen through Sixteen.

People who coach others: Focus on Part Three (Chapters Fourteen through Seventeen).

Organization development consultants: Sorry, you need to read the whole book!

Three Ways to Focus While Reading: Self, Others, and Organization

A knowledge of personality structure, dynamics, and development will be helpful in three primary contexts: your personal professional development, how you relate to your associates, and how you relate to your boss and your organization in general. In the concluding pages of Chapters Two through Six, we guide you in considering specific implications of personality trait patterns for these three areas. In addition, we recommend that you periodically ask the following three questions:

1. *How can this material help me to be more productive and more satisfied at work?* Perhaps you should redesign your job, delegate more or differently, get some training (or mentoring or coaching), ask for reassignment, share jobs with others on your team, change jobs, change industries, or change your career path and goals.

2. *How can this material help me to take a significant relationship to the next level?* Perhaps you and your boss spend inappropriate amounts of time struggling and you want to minimize that struggle. Or you may be in conflict with one or more people who are here to stay and won't go away, and you'd like to try to understand what's going on between you and those people in order to ease the conflict. Or someone at work is presenting an obstacle to your goals and you're losing sleep and growing ulcers from worry over it. This

book may provide you with some insights into better under-standing that person or your job difficulties. Or perhaps you enjoy a particularly fruitful relationship—with your boss or any other associate who's important to you—and you don't want to unintentionally sabotage or derail it. Reading this book may help you to avert a potential disaster.

3. *How can this material help me and others to influence our organizational culture so that it harnesses the right people in the right way for the optimum performance and quality of life of our owners, associates, and customers?* This book can help by potentially giving you answers to the following questions:

- Are you selecting the right people for jobs with high turnover or marginal performance?

- Are your or others' well-intentioned but misguided expectations causing frustration, boredom, and marginal performance?

- Is your research and development strategy aimed at satisfying the unique personality needs of your market segment?

- Is your sales and advertising strategy appropriate for achieving the maximum impact on the unique personality profile of your market segment?

- Do your project and long-term teams have the appropriate mix of personality traits to accomplish their missions effectively?

Periodically ask the three overall questions and shape your answers into an action plan. When no answers are forthcoming, iden-tify a resource (such as *Cent*ACS' global affiliate companies and con-sulting network on our website) to help you find them.

And, Finally, Some Definitions

Words, words, words. Can't live with them, can't live without them! Most of this book is written in everyday, accessible language, yet a few special terms litter the landscape. If we've erred and included an obscure word here or there, we apologize in advance and hope that your favorite dictionary will suffice for clarification.

However, several terms do appear throughout the book that might be confusing. They all really refer to just two concepts: broad categories and subcategories of personality structure. For the most part, the various synonyms we use are perfectly interchangeable, although a couple of subtle differences in meaning do exist.

Broad Categories of Personality Structure

For broad categories, we use the words *trait, dimension, continuum, supertrait, secondary trait, factor,* and *domain.* All of these are interchangeable. *Factor* refers specifically to a broad category (such as Extraversion) that has been arrived at through the statistical procedure called factor analysis. *Secondary traits* are so called because they refer to the fact that factors are comprised of smaller elements, which are called primary traits. *Domain* refers to a broad category that represents the simple averaging of subcategories—for example, the domain of Extraversion (a secondary, or broad, category) would represent the average of its subcategories (also called primary traits), such as warmth, gregariousness, activity level, and assertiveness. *Continuum* emphasizes the aspect of broad categories that represents a scale with two extremes, such as the continua from hot to cold or solitary to gregarious. Each of the Big Five terms is such a broad category.

Subcategories of Personality Structure

For subcategories of personality structure, we use the words *facet, subfactor, primary trait, subtrait,* or, simply, *trait.* Each broad category can be understood in terms of its component parts. Extraversion is comprised of warmth, gregariousness, assertiveness, and so forth. Extraversion is a supertrait, and the others are subtraits. Or we can say that Extraversion is a factor, and the others are facets of that factor.

Notice that we have included the word *trait* in both groups. All recognizable patterns of behavior are called traits, whether they are broader and more inclusive (such as Extraversion) or narrower and more stand-alone (such as gregariousness). Thus it is common to use the word *trait* in both the broad and narrow senses.

That's enough for the preliminaries. Let's now take a look at personality at work.

Part
One

The Why

and

What of

Personality

at Work

Getting to Know You

Setting the Stage

Why Study Personality at Work?

During a typical week, while trying to get our jobs done, each of us runs head-first into personalities. Personalities at work are like cars in the city: they often can keep us from our destination. On the other hand, personalities can also make the job easier. Here are just a few examples of these two effects:

An insensitive manager: Ellen was an award-winning architect and had been managing a team of a dozen architects and project managers for about two years. Everyone in her department, to a person, hated her and complained above her head about her unfair, insensitive management practices. Her boss didn't know how to get to the next level short of firing her.

> **Why is it that I always get a whole person when what I really want is a pair of hands?**
>
> —*Henry Ford*

A model employee: Tomas was the number-one border patrol agent in the Drug Enforcement Agency. He consistently had the highest arrest rate and could do no wrong, and the powers-that-be wanted to clone him. How did he do this?

A team that was breaking down: A training team delivered top-notch programs to the thirty-campus health care conglomerate for which it was responsible. However, team meetings typically ran over by several hours, members resented the intrusion into their private planning time, and their respect for their team leader and each other was eroding.

Fighting managers: Jon and Fran managed two different manufacturing processes housed under one common roof. Jon's bottom line looked great, but sales were stagnant; Fran's margins were nonexistent, but sales were soaring. They were at each other's throats daily, and their boss had no clue how to resolve their backbiting, destructive conflict, blaming, and lack of mutual respect.

A lawyer who hated her job: Heminway was a successful litigant who had grown to hate the law. At age forty, she was rolling in money, but sleepless. She dreaded the thought of going to court another day.

Personality and the Bottom Line

The bottom line in these examples is performance, for the individual and the company. Understanding your own personality better as well as the personalities of those you work with can make a significant difference in your performance and advancement. The way you communicate, persuade, and motivate is important if you are working on a team, leading a department, or selling a service or product. Much of your success may depend on how well you understand and act on the personality dynamics in your workplace.

Whether you're a vice president of a division, a professional who has no staff, or a customer service representative, you have company goals to achieve. Your ability to understand the personalities of the people you work with and those of your customers or clients plays a big part in how quickly and effectively you can achieve the functions for which you're responsible.

We wrote this book so that you can better understand how personality can both obstruct and enhance work. Before you reach the end of the book, you'll be able to name the traits responsible for each of the dilemmas just described, understand the dynamics that contributed to the problem, and identify strategies for getting to the next level. To help you do this, at the end of each of the next five chapters, we have included implications of the Big Five personality dimensions for your performance and that of your associates.

What Is the Big Five Model?

The terms *Big Five* and *Five-Factor Model* are, for our purposes, interchangeable. The model emerged from a line of research begun in 1936 when Gordon Allport and Harold Odbert threw out a challenge to the psychological research community. They had identified approximately 18,000 words in the unabridged English dictionary that described personality. After paring away some 13,500 words because they didn't portray normal everyday personality characteristics, Allport and Odbert (1936, p. 24) suggested that psychological researchers determine how many synonym clusters were required "to distinguish the behavior of one human being from that of another." After a long line of research (see the time line in the appendix), a solution was finally reached in the 1980s. Why so long? Early solutions were based on factor analyses that were done manually and were full of errors. The invention of the personal computer and the availability of factor analysis software enabled a flurry of research in the early 1980s to converge on a common solution.

The answer? Five synonym clusters appear to account for the majority of the differences between individual personalities. Today, these five factors are typically referred to by the five letters *N, E, O, A,* and *C.* Although different names are sometimes given to the five factors by different researchers (sometimes for academic reasons, sometimes for marketing ones!), N, E, O, A, and C always refer to the same personality dimensions, regardless of what the actual names are. These five basic dimensions are summarized in Figure 1.1.

N refers to one's "Need for Stability," or "Negative Emotionality." A person high in N is very reactive and prefers a stress-free workplace, while a person low in N is very calm and is relatively unaffected by stress that might cripple others.

N	**NEED FOR STABILITY** **NEGATIVE EMOTIONALITY** **NEUROTICISM**		
	Low scorers	**Midrange scorers**	**High scorers**
	Resilient (content, controlled, secure, stress-free)	*Responsive* (occasionally bothered by stressful circumstances)	*Reactive* (tense, alert, anxious)
E	**EXTRAVERSION** **POSITIVE EMOTIONALITY** **SOCIABILITY**		
	Low scorers	**Midrange scorers**	**High scorers**
	Introvert (private, reserved, inhibited)	*Ambivert* (enjoys a balance of solitude and sociability)	*Extravert* (sociable, enthusiastic, active)
O	**ORIGINALITY** **OPENNESS TO EXPERIENCE** **IMAGINATION**		
	Low scorers	**Midrange scorers**	**High scorers**
	Preserver (conservative, practical, efficient)	*Moderate* (good managing the tension between innovation and efficiency)	*Explorer* (curious, dreamer, visionary)
A	**ACCOMMODATION** **AGREEABLENESS** **ADAPTABILITY**		
	Low scorers	**Midrange scorers**	**High scorers**
	Challenger (questioning, competitive, proud)	*Negotiator* (comfortable holding out for the win-win situation)	*Adapter* (accepting, good as a team player, serving, helping)
C	**CONSOLIDATION** **CONSCIENTIOUSNESS** **WILL TO ACHIEVE**		
	Low scorers	**Midrange scorers**	**High scorers**
	Flexible (spontaneous, playful, comfortable with chaos, good at multitasking)	*Balanced* (keeps work and private demands in balance)	*Focused* (organized, perfectionistic, ambitious)

FIGURE 1.1 *The Big Five Personality Dimensions.*

E refers to one's "Extraversion." A person high in E likes to be in the thick of the action, while a person low in E likes to be away from the noise and hubbub.

O refers to one's "Originality," or "Openness to Experience." A person high in O has a voracious appetite for new ideas and activities and is easily bored, while a person low in O prefers familiar territory and tends to be more practical.

A refers to one's "Accommodation," or "Agreeableness." A person high in A has a tendency to accommodate to the wishes and needs of others, while a person low in A tends to cater to his or her own personal priorities.

C refers to one's "Consolidation," or "Conscientiousness." A person high in C tends to consolidate her or his energy and resources on accomplishing one or more goals, while a person low in C prefers a more spontaneous work style that involves switching from one task to another.

The next five chapters go into greater depth in defining these five basic dimensions.

How Do We Know This Model Is Any Good?

The psychological community has reached near consensus on the validity of the Five-Factor Model. Digman and Inouye (1986, p. 116) call it "a finding consistent enough to approach the status of law." This should tell those of us in the business world that, finally, a standard vocabulary is available with which to discuss individual differences. In the past, a virtual alphabet soup was used in selection, training, coaching, and all manner of human resource development applications. You may have taken some of these tests. Why, after so many different models have been proposed and dissected, do psychologists affirm the Big Five? Here are some of the reasons:

- *Reliability:* The coefficient alpha statistic hovers around .90 for the long forms of Big Five tests, around .80 for the shorter forms. This unprecedented high level of reliability offers a consistency of measurement that is extremely attractive to a business environment that cherishes continual improvement and high quality.

- *Validity:* The Five-Factor Model has demonstrated an impressive ability to predict future performance. In classic studies such as one done by Barrick and Mount (1991), Big Five traits show clear associations with a variety of job types. This stands in contrast to the popular Myers-Briggs Type Indicator, whose validity has suffered severe attacks in the last decade (see McCrae and Costa, 1989).

- *Norms:* The commonly accepted standard measure of the Big Five, Costa and McCrae's NEO PI-R (1992), is based on 500 men and 500 women pulled randomly from three different well-respected studies done in connection with Costa and McCrae's work with the Baltimore Longitudinal Study of Aging, which is a part of the National Institute on Aging of the National Institutes of Health; it is housed at The Johns Hopkins University in Baltimore, Maryland.

- *Global applicability:* The Five-Factor Model has held up in a variety of national, economic, cultural, religious, and linguistic settings, including versions in English, Spanish, Italian, German, Portuguese, Dutch, Chinese, Japanese, Korean, Hebrew, Turkish, Shone, Finnish, Swedish, Czech, Polish, Russian, French, Norwegian, Hungarian, Icelandic, and Taiwanese.

- *Descriptive power:* The Big Five model has facilitated the unearthing of new knowledge about personality, such as the discovery that N, E, and O decrease measurably from age twenty to age thirty (that is, we become less reactive, sociable, and curious) and A and C increase during the same period (that is, we become more team-oriented and ambitious). This relationship, which is crucial to understanding what happens to candidates we bring into the workforce in their early twenties, is portrayed in Figure 1.2.

How This Book Is Organized

Okay, so we know it's good! How do we proceed? The remainder of Part One provides in-depth definitions and examples of the Big Five personality dimensions in the workplace. Part Two shows you how to use the Big Five profiles in a variety of contexts, including sales, leadership, and teams. Part Three provides a somewhat more theoretical slant on how to regard and use the Big

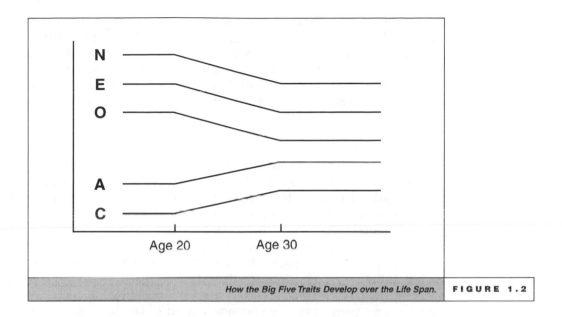

How the Big Five Traits Develop over the Life Span.　FIGURE 1.2

Five. Don't grimace! This theory stuff is actually very basic and hands-on. It treats the nature-nurture debate and its implications for the development of competency in your professional performance. As we have been advised by organizational researcher Rensis Likert, "There is nothing so useful as a good theory!"

Developing a Model for the Workplace

This book is based on the Five-Factor Model, but you should be aware that dozens of tests are available for measuring this model. While the most highly regarded standard test for measuring the Big Five is Costa and McCrae's NEO PI-R (or, more simply, the NEO), it became apparent to us that a need existed for a five-factor instrument that was designed with only the workplace in mind. We began development of such a test, and in the fall of 2000 we introduced the WorkPlace Big Five ProFile (or, more simply, the WB5P), which featured questions and reports that used the language of the workplace.

Keeping the basic tradition established in the 1980s, we referred to the five factors as *N, E, O, A,* and *C,* but we changed the terminology to reflect the needs of the workplace. In addition, we found that several of the NEO facets were unnecessary in workplace applications such as coaching, selection, and team building, so the new model discontinued these facets. Also, after scanning other Big Five instruments, we identified several facets that weren't included in the NEO but were important in the workplace. These two versions of the Five-Factor Model are compared in Table 1.1. In the table, two entries that are on the same line can be considered parallel constructs. An entry in only one column indicates that the construct has no parallel in the other model.

The letters N, E, O, A, and C refer to the same supertrait whether you are using the NEO or the WB5P. For example, A always refers to the dimension that contains Challengers, Negotiators, and Adapters. Whether we call the dimension Agreeableness or Accommodation doesn't matter. The two labels refer to the same construct. A Challenger may be described as "low in Agreeableness" or "low in Accommodation": both mean the same thing. We have changed the names of the five dimensions for the WB5P so that they sound less value-laden and more businesslike. Extraversion is the only name we didn't change, because it is commonly used in the workplace and doesn't have the same socially desirable (or undesirable) values associated with it as Negative Emotionality, Openness, Agreeableness, and Conscientiousness.

Most of the subtraits in each model also have clear parallels in both work and private life: for example, anger (NEO) and intensity (WorkPlace), warmth (NEO) and enthusiasm (WorkPlace), fantasy (NEO) and imagination (WorkPlace), self-discipline (NEO) and concentration (WorkPlace). Each of these pairs of traits, while having different names, has the same underlying construct. The construct underlying the terms "sensitiveness" and "anxiety" is the tendency to experience the fear that events might go awry, that the future may not be bright, but the label "sensitiveness" seems to more appropriately describe its appearance in the workplace (for example, a customer service representative might be "sensitive" about the resolution of a customer's issues), while "anxiety" seems more appropriate in describing such personal fears in private life. Nevertheless, the behaviors associated with either label are the same, whether they crop up in the workplace or in the home.

However, some of the NEO subtraits are not appropriate to use in describing the workplace personality, and some of the WorkPlace subtraits are not appropriate to use when taking a more generic look

The Big Five Factors, with Facets of the WorkPlace Big Five ProFile and NEO PI-R Models.	**TABLE 1.1**

WorkPlace Model	NEO Model
N: Need for Stability N1: Sensitiveness N2: Intensity N3: Interpretation (includes NEO's E6) N4: Rebound time	**N: Negative Emotionality** N1: Worry N2: Anger N3: Discouragement N4: Self-consciousness (A5 on WB5P) N5: Impulsiveness N6: Vulnerability
E: Extraversion E1: Enthusiasm E2: Sociability E3: Energy mode E4: Taking charge E5: Trust of others (A1 on NEO) E6: Tact (A2 on NEO, reversed)	**E: Extraversion** E1: Warmth E2: Gregariousness E3: Assertiveness (A4 on WB5P, reversed) E4: Activity E5: Excitement seeking E6: Positive emotions (part of N3 in WB5P)
O: Originality O1: Imagination O2: Complexity O3: Change O4: Scope	**O: Openness** O1: Fantasy O2: Aesthetics O3: Feelings O5: Ideas O4: Actions O6: Values
A: Accommodation A1: Service (combines NEO A3 and A6) A2: Agreement A3: Deference A4: Reserve (E3 on NEO, reversed) A5: Reticence (N4 on NEO)	**A: Agreeableness** A1: Trust (E5 on WB5P) A2: Straightforwardness (E6 on WB5P, reversed) A3: Altruism A6: Tender-mindedness A4: Compliance A5: Modesty
C: Consolidation C1: Perfectionism C2: Organization C3: Drive C4: Concentration C5: Methodicalness	**C: Conscientiousness** C1: Competence C2: Order C3: Dutifulness C4: Achievement striving C5: Self-discipline C6: Deliberation

at personality. For example, the NEO measures urge control (impulsiveness), aesthetics, and values. Urge control (the N5 facet) and values (the O6 facet) are of a more personal nature and are minimal, if not absent, in the value they provide for understanding workplace behavior. We don't need to ask (and shouldn't) whether a prospective employee eats too much or is a political or religious liberal. Aesthetics (the O2 facet) also provides no job-related information. For architects, perhaps, but they wouldn't be architects if they weren't aesthetic. On the other hand, taking charge (the E4 facet) and scope (the O4 facet) on the WorkPlace instrument are of no particular interest away from the workplace. The first deals with a willingness to take on supervisory responsibilities and the other with a preference for handling repetitive details as opposed to working more with the big picture. Both of these traits are more reflective of the workplace than of private life.

Although we can use either the WB5P or the NEO to measure the Five-Factor Model, the instrument we use depends on the use we have in mind for it. The NEO is used for describing the generic adult personality, both on and off the job, whereas the WorkPlace is used only for describing adult personality in the workplace. Because of this, we will use the WorkPlace terms throughout this book, unless we specify NEO terms.

The Concept of a Continuum

Each of the five supertraits (and its subtraits) forms a continuum. For example, imagine that we're talking about how hungry you are. Now convert your level of hunger into a 100-point scale. Define 0 on your scale as the area where you're so hungry that your stomach is growling repeatedly, your blood sugar level is dropping, and you feel that you must find something to eat immediately. Next, define 100 on your imaginary scale as the saturation limit, where you're completely full and feel that you simply can't eat another bite without making yourself literally sick. With your 100-point scale or continuum firmly in mind, decide how hungry you are at this moment. Are you just beginning to think that you'll need to eat in an hour or so? Maybe that would translate into a score of 40 on your imaginary scale. Or are you still comfortably full from eating your last meal? That feeling might translate into a score of 75. If you're neither hungry nor full, you might equate this midrange level to a score of 50. This mental exercise with your hunger level should give you an idea of how the continuum works. (Of course, it may send you elsewhere in search of a snack!)

Based on the way test makers have constructed the 100-point trait scales, a little over one-third of the population will score in the midrange, between 45 and 55; just under one-third will score above 55; and another third will score below 45. This distribution is presented in Figure 1.3. Obviously, hunger is not the same thing as personality. For one thing, hunger changes hourly throughout the day, whereas adult personality remains fairly stable. Someone who scores extremely high on A will exhibit the behaviors and characteristics associated with the high endpoint of the A continuum most of the time: he or she will usually be an agreeable team player who accommodates other people. Yet occasionally, even those who score at one endpoint may show behaviors or characteristics associated with the other end of the scale; people who are high in A, for example, will occasionally stand up for themselves and challenge others. Someone who scores in the midrange between 45 and 55 may alternate fairly equally between the behaviors and characteristics associated with scores near the endpoints of the continuum, seeming to balance between them. A person who scores 50 on A, for example, is more likely to exhibit a balance of challenging and accommodating behaviors, believing that "you win some, you lose some." We will consider some exceptions to these rules in Chapter Seven.

How the Letters and Signs Work

Throughout this book, we'll refer to the traits with letters and signs. It may take a chapter or two for you to get the hang of it, but we'll offer reminders in the margins of the pages. Five signs and five letters. That's it. Each continuum (see Figure 1.3) is, in essence, divided into five sections, with a very high score (above 65) represented by two plus signs (++), a moderately high score (between 55 and 65) by one plus sign (+), a midrange score (between 45 and 55) by the equal sign (=), a moderately low score (between 35 and 45) by one minus sign (–), and a very low score (below 35) by two minus signs (– –). So E++ refers to someone who is very extraverted—a consummate salesperson who is very enthusiastic, very sociable, and very active. Likewise, A= would refer to someone who is in the midrange in Agreeableness/Accommodation, some-

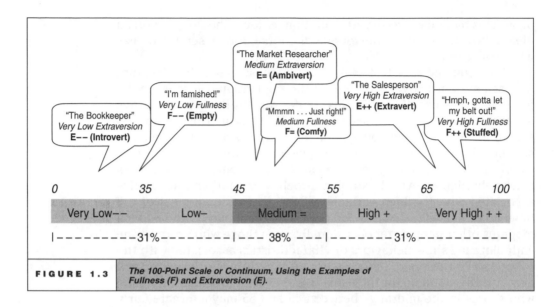

| FIGURE 1.3 | *The 100-Point Scale or Continuum, Using the Examples of Fullness (F) and Extraversion (E).* |

one who leans toward neither challenging (A– or A––) nor adapting (A+ or A++), a negotiator who is comfortable working toward a win-win situation. A person who is N–– would be very calm and at ease and have nerves of steel, as would be true of a pilot or surgeon. The difference between a C+ and a C++ executive would be that one is focused and hardworking (C+) and the other is *compulsively* focused and hardworking, a workaholic (C++). Got it? Good!

Estimating and Remembering Your Personal Profile

Now turn to the back cover of the book and pull out the inside fold. After you've opened it out, you'll see that it's entitled "Your Big Five Profile Estimate." If you leave it folded out, you'll be able to refer to it while reading the rest of the book. It will serve as a reminder of the trait definitions as well as showing you how you fit into the model. Take some time at the end of the next five chapters to estimate whether you belong in the very high (++), high (+), midrange (=), low (–), or very low (––) range of each of the Big Five traits. If you already know your scores from having taken a Big Five instrument, enter them on the pullout now.

A Word of Caution

We wish to emphasize one point before delving into definitions and examples. Human personality is complex, mysterious, and wonderful. Even though we have agreed upon five super-traits, we haven't unlocked the mystery of personality; we've merely found a uniform language to use in our exploration. Having the building blocks of personality in hand doesn't allow us to make an individual. N, E, O, A, and C are to the individual as sugar, flour, eggs, and milk are to cookies. The ingredients are not the same as the final product. And we must remember that having a uniform language to describe individuals does not indicate that there's any one right way to be or any one profile that represents an ideal. As Ralph Waldo Emerson reminds us, "Every individual nature has its own beauty."

Many forces are at work in shaping the individual, with the five factors forming only the main infrastructure. If there were only ten personality traits, with ten levels of each trait, we'd be able to describe some ten billion unique combinations. In fact, over two dozen different traits are subsumed under the Big Five, providing for literally trillions of combinations. In his book *The Roots of the Self,* Robert Ornstein (1993, p. 4) wrote: "So don't expect to discover in these pages a formula for finding yourself. It just can't be done. Consider this: at any mating, one male and one female could produce 52 trillion biologically distinct individuals. . . . Simply put, human individuality is genetically too complex for any one system to explain."

But just because perfect knowledge of ourselves and others is impossible, that doesn't mean we shouldn't endeavor to build that knowledge. As Stephen Jay Gould wrote in *Eight Little Piggies* (1993), "Details are all that matters. God dwells there, and you never see Him if you don't struggle to get them right." Let us now start the struggle, together, and catch a glimpse of the wonder of human personality at work.

If you haven't read the Introduction yet, please do so now before beginning Chapter Two. We know that, realistically speaking, most of us skip book introductions in our eagerness to get to the "real" content. However, we'd be remiss if we didn't point out to you that the Introduction contains important information about the way to approach our Big Five material. It provides tips for the several different kinds of readers who've found their way here, highlights the specific chapters that are most relevant to particular jobs, includes guidelines and questions to help you focus on aspects of the book that may be of special interest to you, and contains the definitions for the multitude of personality terms that are used throughout the next eighteen chapters.

N Stress

Need for Stability/ Negative Emotionality

+

Nerves provide me with energy. They work for me. It's when I don't have them, when I feel at ease, that I get worried.

—Mike Nichols

=

To despise the animal basis of life, to seek value only at the level of conscious intelligence and rational effort, is ultimately to lose one's sense of cosmic relationships.

—Lewis Mumford

Nothing gives one person so much advantage over another as to remain always cool and unruffled under all circumstances.

—Thomas Jefferson

41

Three statements that introduce this chapter are samples of how an individual speaks who is thinking and feeling in accordance with the higher, medium, or lower regions of the N continuum. Speaking in this manner doesn't necessarily imply that a person will stay in that area of the continuum all of the time. Thomas Jefferson speaks of the value of cool rationality, but he may not always have been coolly rational. His rapture with Sally Hemings was proof that he could behave according to *both* ends of the N continuum—in control *as well as* out of control. These quotes are not intended to identify the speaker as definitely possessing the trait expressed in the quote, only to illustrate the meaning of the quote.

All of the quotes are meant to portray positive behaviors. While a quote may *sound* negative or undesirable in some way, that's probably because it differs from how you personally might feel or think. In the proper context, the quotes are all healthy, positive, productive, and desirable. We all demonstrate behaviors at both ends of each continuum—we both cry (N+) and reason (N–); commenting on one of the behaviors doesn't necessarily mean that we endorse the behavior. The statement "If men could cry, then they could love" doesn't imply that the speaker is N+ or N–, only that she or he is talking about an N+ behavior: crying.

The Biological Basis for Stress

Each of the Big Five traits reflects the physiological activity of an underlying arousal system. In each case, a unique type of stimulus triggers the arousal system into action. For N (Need for Stability, or Negative Emotionality), the arousal system involved is the autonomic nervous system. The stimulus that triggers it is stress, which elicits the *general adaptation syndrome,* or the *fight-or-flight response.* Thus, in a sense, your N score is an estimate of the point at which your fight-or-flight response is triggered and your body moves into autonomic arousal and the activation of the sympathetic nervous system. This period of arousal is eventually counterbalanced by parasympathetic arousal, or a return to normalcy and calmness. Individuals with higher scores (N+ and N++) have a shorter "trigger" and can't take very much stress before feeling it. Those with lower scores (N– and N– –) have a lot of "play" in their stress trigger and are able to take abundant amounts of stress before feeling and showing symptoms of stress: they are often described as having "ice water in their veins." Individuals with moderate scores (=) are literally in between, unable to take as much stress as people at one extreme but able to take more than those at the other extreme.

Let's now take a closer look at the types of behavior associated with the three areas of the N dimension.

Resilient (N–)

If you are a Resilient, you tend to respond to stressful situations in a calm, secure, steady, and rational way. Typically, you are stress-free, guilt-free, and urge-resistant. Unless you are very attentive, you may appear to others to be too laid back and relaxed; to be uncaring, lethargic, insensitive, or unaware of the seriousness of problems; or to have tunnel vision. You may not take stressful situations or problems as seriously as you should, because you can usually manage without too many difficulties even when the stress is occurring all around you. As problems arise, you typically move into a problem-solving mode rather rapidly and proceed in a rational, analytic way until the problem or the source of the stress has been handled.

Responsive (N=)

If you are a Responsive, you tend to be calm, secure, and steady under normal circumstances. However, surprises, pressures, emergencies, difficult situations, or stressful circumstances can sometimes lead you to worry, anger, depression, discouragement, or other types of stressful responses. Basically, you have a moderate threshold for handling stress in the workplace. When difficulties arise, you may need a moment or two to blow off steam or get over your disappointment before resuming your regular activities or moving into a problem-solving mode.

Reactive (N+)

If you are a Reactive, you tend to respond to most situations in an alert, sensitive, concerned, attentive, excitable, or expressive way. Under stress, you may be perceived by others as

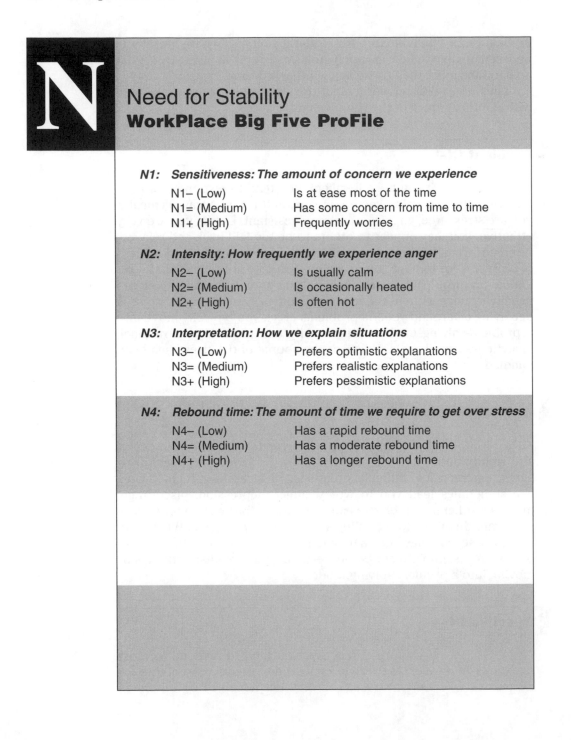

N

Need for Stability
WorkPlace Big Five ProFile

N1:   Sensitiveness: The amount of concern we experience

N1– (Low)	Is at ease most of the time
N1= (Medium)	Has some concern from time to time
N1+ (High)	Frequently worries

N2:   Intensity: How frequently we experience anger

N2– (Low)	Is usually calm
N2= (Medium)	Is occasionally heated
N2+ (High)	Is often hot

N3:   Interpretation: How we explain situations

N3– (Low)	Prefers optimistic explanations
N3= (Medium)	Prefers realistic explanations
N3+ (High)	Prefers pessimistic explanations

N4:   Rebound time: The amount of time we require to get over stress

N4– (Low)	Has a rapid rebound time
N4= (Medium)	Has a moderate rebound time
N4+ (High)	Has a longer rebound time

Negative Emotionality
NEO PI-R

N

N1: *Worry: Worry and fear about how things will turn out*

N1– (Low)	Is relaxed, calm, unconcerned
N1= (Medium)	Is usually calm, sometimes worries
N1+ (High)	Worries, is uneasy

N2: *Anger: How quickly we come to feel anger and bitterness*

N2– (Low)	Is composed, slow to anger
N2= (Medium)	Is seldom angry, but can be provoked
N2+ (High)	Is quick to feel anger

N3: *Discouragement: Our tendency to feel sad and hopeless*

N3– (Low)	Is rarely discouraged, guilt free
N3= (Medium)	Is sensitive to losing, but recovers well
N3+ (Low)	Is easily discouraged

N4: *Self-consciousness: Embarrassment or shame at awkward public situations*

N4– (Low)	Is hard to embarrass, status-free
N4= (Medium)	Gets embarrassed, then gets over it
N4+ (High)	Is more easily embarrassed

N5: *Impulsiveness: The tendency to yield to temptation (food, drink, tobacco, drugs, shopping, and so on)*

N5– (Low)	Resists urges easily, is not excitable
N5= (Medium)	Sometimes yields, but rarely to excess
N5+ (High)	Is easily tempted, is excitable

N6: *Vulnerability: The tendency to lose focus in emergency or stressful situations; the tendency to be panic-prone*

N6– (Low)	Handles stress and crises well
N6= (Medium)	Experiences stress, but copes effectively
N6+ (High)	Has difficulty coping, feels vulnerable

being anxious, tense, restless, depressed, easily discouraged, temperamental, or worried. Typically, you feel the effect of even a little workplace stress more readily than most people and often serve as the "conscience" of those around you. When problems or difficult situations arise, you may tend to take them personally, thinking of them as your problems to solve or as your responsibility even if they really belong to or were caused by someone else. In tough times, you may need plenty of time to vent your frustrations or get over your concerns before you're ready to tackle the next job challenge.

The N Facets with Definitions

Using the WorkPlace Big Five ProFile, we have measured four facet scales within Need for Stability. If we use the NEO PI-R facets, we can measure six separate facets within N, the scale we refer to as Negative Emotionality. Their definitions are given on pages 44–45, along with anchors (descriptive phrases) for the high, midrange, and low ranges of each facet's continuum.

N Case Study 1
The Customer Problem

In the workplace, some of the dynamics that occur between low-, mid-, and high-scoring team members on the N dimension can be classically illustrated by the following situation. The Reactive subordinate (N+), concerned about a problem with a customer, rushes into the office of the Resilient boss (N–), where he exclaims, "Oh my gosh! We've got a real problem with the XYZ Company! They've threatened that if we don't take action now on this morning's product complaint, they'll take their account to our biggest competitor. We need to call the team together immediately to discuss what we're going to do!"

The Resilient boss (N–) calmly rolls her eyes toward the Responsive (N=), another subordinate, who happens to be in her office. The boss calmly says to the Reactive (N+), "Now Bill, you just need to chill a bit. Yes, XYZ threatens to pull their account away every other day over any minor little difficulty. It's just their way to get quick action and to get us to hop when they say 'frog.' Calm down and we'll get back to them after lunch."

The Responsive subordinate (N=) squirms a little uncomfortably in her chair and says, "Well, I think we shouldn't wait too long to respond. One of the main reasons XYZ originally gave us their business was that we guaranteed them a prompt response to any product problems anytime. Putting them off until this afternoon could affect our company's business relationship with them. This is probably a minor problem, but I think we need to deal with it within the next hour or so and get back to our customer. Bill, I think you're right to bring it to our attention at this time."

This story emphasizes that people who score in the midrange and higher in N (N= and N+) tend to take the concerns of their workplace customers more seriously. Often people who score lower in N (N–) don't take the concerns of their customers seriously enough. This difference in the level of seriousness can apply to both the internal and external customers we deal with in our daily work. In the overall workplace, however, we need both the calming force of the N–, the strong ownership and sense of conscience about problems of the N+, and the equalizing efforts of the N= in order to accomplish our daily work.

N Case Study 2
The Late Overview

At a leadership retreat in the North Carolina mountain getaway called Wildacres, fifty executives were presented with this situation: "You have just picked up your office telephone to hear the voice of a boss two levels above you in your organization angrily saying, 'Where in the heck are you? You were supposed to be here ten minutes ago to do an overview for my senior management team.' Without talking to anyone, write down what you're thinking or feeling at this very moment."

The spokesman for the N−− group (those who scored 34 or lower on the N scale) calmly stood up and said that he would get the appropriate file and go to the meeting or ask if the boss wanted to reschedule the meeting for another time.

The spokeswoman for the N− group (35–44) said that they felt a little anxious about the situation but were sure that someone had forgotten to tell them about the meeting. However, they would collect their materials and go to the meeting.

A spokesman for the N= midrange scorers (45–55) looked a little shy about having to make a public presentation to the room of fifty people but appeared to become more comfortable and spoke more strongly as he continued. He told us that his group was worried and anxious about how the boss might feel toward them and said that they had debated about whether they'd failed to put the meeting on their calendar or whether someone else had made the error. They had also decided that the boss was overreacting and probably shouldn't have spoken so angrily on the phone. In any event, as soon as the boss had called, they had decided to grab their information and go to the meeting. When they arrived at the meeting, they'd decide whether they needed to make a verbal apology.

The woman who spoke for the N+ range (56–65) looked somewhat ill at ease in front of the large gathering and her voice wavered slightly as she spoke, but her tone of voice was strong and full of the emotion that she obviously felt. She said that her group had talked about feeling physically uncomfortable after receiving the phone call from the boss. They used descriptive words such as "very anxious," "very worried," and "really scared" and included a few expletives. The group members thought that they were the ones who had personally erred in not putting the meeting on their calendars. Their plan was to go immediately to the meeting and apologize for being late. They also said that they'd probably speak directly to the boss later and apologize again.

The spokesman for the N++ group (66–100) looked decidedly reluctant to stand up and face the room of fifty people. He shifted from foot to foot throughout his presentation and mainly looked down at his notes or around to his group members for support, yet his verbal comments were full of passion and emotion. He said that they were mortified by the situation with their boss, felt sick, and were sure that their careers would be ruined from this point forward. They knew that they'd personally "screwed up" by not putting the meeting on their calendars. They said that they would immediately dash to the meeting, then would make profuse apologies to the boss and the other people present, while telling themselves mentally that they should just accept the fact that they were going to be fired for this major mistake and should start working on their résumés.

In reflecting on the different reports, one of the main elements the participants noticed was how personally the higher-scoring groups seemed to take the situation. The perception of the communication error shifted from being someone else's fault with the lower-scoring groups to being a personal, career-altering mistake with the higher-scoring groups.

Another difference they noticed was the level of emotion or passion that emerged from the speakers as they moved up the scale. In fact, several minutes into the small-group portion of the exercise, the N−− group asked us what was taking the N+ and N++ groups so long. They also had noticed strong gestures and expressions coming from the higher-scoring groups. The lower scorers, N−− and N−, had quickly and rationally handled their discussions of the situation and were ready to present, while the higher-scoring groups needed to vent and talk through their emotional and personal responses to the stressful situation before they could begin to move into a problem-solving mode in order to determine what they actually needed to do.

The N+ and N++ groups couldn't understand the calm, laid-back approach taken by the N− and N−− groups, while the N= group admitted that they had experienced a combination of the feelings and emotions being voiced by both the N− and N+ groups. During the discussion, one man in the N++ group looked at the N−− group and said, "I've got a boss like you guys. He's always calm, cool, rational—really frustrating. One time, when I made a major mistake that inconvenienced him, I sent him an apology card. When he got it, he just laughed and told my co-workers about it. They laughed too, and I felt really embarrassed about the whole situation. Should I have just let the whole situation blow over without doing anything or apologizing?" At this point in the discussion, the members of the N−− group looked back at the N++ person and in unison, without much expression, said, "Yep." The N= group found this very amusing and came up with even more questions about the situation.

N Case Study 3
The Banking Managers

In the late 1990s, we had the opportunity to work with a group of fourteen midlevel managers in one of the top ten banks in the United States. The managers were diverse in gender, race, and age. Although they formed an intact team and were accustomed to working together, they were geographically dispersed and lacked the benefit of daily contact. For the team-building session we were to lead, we gathered in a centrally located U.S. city; the managers flew in from regions throughout the country for the session.

Prior to the two-day session, we had administered the Big Five to the managers so that we could provide them with complete, detailed information about their personalities during the team-building session. As the participants entered the conference room where the session was to be held, we greeted each one. Lunch was being served in the room, so as people arrived from their flights, they were busy getting served, eating, and talking to their team members, whom they saw infrequently in person at quarterly meetings such as this one. One of the people we greeted during the welcoming process was a woman whose name we recognized immediately. We had been looking for her so we could talk with her briefly before the meeting, just to prepare her for her N score. After she had greeted the people who were already there and apologized to them for running late, we unobtrusively asked her to step away from the milling group to talk with us. We explained to her that we just wanted to let her know about one of her scores on the personality instrument before we started the team-building session (her N score was 79, in the very high range). We assured her that she was normal but that she probably experienced more stress than the other team members and probably more than most people she knew. She looked at us strangely and said, "How did you know that? I usually wonder what's wrong with me. I just can't seem to take life and work as casually as my co-workers do." After a quick discussion and plenty of reassurance, the three of us returned to the rest of the team.

As we began the session, we went through the usual introductory material and then led the banking team through the same situation with the angry boss on the telephone that we had proposed to the leadership retreat group of fifty. The responses throughout this team were similar to those related in N Case Study 2. After hearing their responses and processing them the same way we had with the earlier group, we asked another leading question of this intact work team: how this scale and their scores related to their work as a team within the bank. One of the first responses to our question came from a man who scored N=. He looked at the woman who'd received the score of 79 and said, "I had no idea you were that high. I don't see you as stressed at all; you're always taking on extra projects for the team from all of us. You respond well and rapidly when I have problems, so how does this score make any sense to you?"

Shaking her head slowly, the N++ woman replied, "You just don't know. When we have a work problem, I handle it, but I get all tied up in knots. Then my husband has to hear about it when I get home." She then gave one of the best metaphors we've heard to describe what an N++ feels like most of the time. She said, "I feel like I'm a duck sailing across a lake and leaving a smooth wake. All you see is efficiency in my work and everything under control above the waterline. What I really feel is that I'm paddling fast and furious below the water just to keep myself afloat and to keep going."

Because we'd used the Big Five with this team and because of what this woman told her teammates, they suddenly realized that they'd been dumping all kinds of extra work on her that they didn't want to do, because she would take it on. In fact, during the discussion that followed, she indicated that she would feel guilty or as if she were letting them down if she didn't take on everything asked of her by her teammates. After that realization in the team-building meeting, the team revised the distribution of the overall team workload and gave the N++ woman some well-needed relief.

A month after the session, the woman telephoned us to thank us for helping to relieve some of her stress. We explained that we hadn't relieved the stress; her teammates had. All we'd done in the session was to give them the Big Five as a vocabulary for talking about their individual differences and to facilitate their discussion. By understanding and appreciating the differences in their individual personalities, the team members began to achieve better work performance: their awareness of this woman's stress helped them to deploy her strengths more effectively. Once we can appreciate the fact that diversity is also associated with personality, we can consciously work toward achieving personality diversity in our teams.

IMPLICATIONS FOR YOUR JOB AND CAREER

If you are N–, you stand out from the pack in your ability to perform calmly in high-stress situations. By volunteering for stressful assignments to the degree that makes sense to you, you will be building on your strengths.

If you are N+, you need to seek out a position or role that's essentially stress-free or has only occasional stress. Celebrate your stressful responses, however, because they tend to serve as a conscience, or emotional barometer, for your team or organization.

If you are N=, you'll probably be much more satisfied in the long term if your work includes a balance of stressful and restful episodes. One crisis after another or one deadline on the heels of another will probably be unpleasant for you and, in the long term, will be harmful to your health. You need one of two situations: times of intense stress alternating with times of calm or a regular diet of only moderately stressful situations. You should exercise just after particularly stressful episodes in order to burn up the cortisol (the "fight-or-flight" chemical fuel) that is left in your system from the stress response.

IMPLICATIONS FOR YOUR BOSS AND ASSOCIATES

If you are N– and your boss or associates are N+, you need to take their concerns more seriously if you intend to keep your job and maintain your good relationships. If you appear too laid-back, especially to your boss's concerns, you may find yourself with a surprising response on your performance reviews mentioning your "lack of caring" or "lack of problem ownership."

If you are N+ and have an N– boss, you may find yourself receiving performance reviews that urge you to "calm down," "chill out," or "lighten up." The boss may tell you that you're being far too serious and overreacting to problems.

If you score N= and have a boss or associate who's similar to you, you may find that your level of seriousness or your response to customers is exactly right. The same is true if you and your boss or associate are both N– or are both N+. People who are similar to us tend to make us more comfortable, because they understand how we think and how we approach problems.

Before beginning the next chapter, make sure that you have entered your best estimate of your N score on the pullout profile that is part of the back cover of this book.

E Sociability

Extraversion

+

66 Good company and good discourse are the very sinews of virtue. 99

—Izaak Walton

=

66 Solitude and company may be allowed to take their turns: the one creates in us the love of mankind, the other that of ourselves; solitude relieves us when we are sick of company, and conversation when we are weary of being alone, so that the one cures the other. There is no man so miserable as he that is at a loss how to use his time. 99

—Seneca

66 The strongest man in the world is he who stands most alone. 99

—Henrik Ibsen

bsen nails the essence of what we're like when we introvert: we prefer to be alone. Typically, aloneness entails quiet, solitude, stillness—in general, the absence of sensory stimulation. When we extravert, we resemble more Izaak Walton's evoked portrait of crowds, talk, and a party for the five senses. Many of us find it unpleasant to experience too much of either of these extremes; we are considered to be more "ambiverted." As Seneca phrases it, the extremes "take their turns." With some Ambiverts, the extremes may never occur, whereas others show a preference for moderate stimulation and moderate companionship, rejecting both crowds and solitude.

The Biological Basis for Sociability

If the arousal system for N is the autonomic nervous system, with alternating sympathetic and parasympathetic arousal, then the arousal system for E is the motoric nervous system, with alternating afferent and efferent nerves receiving and sending sensory impulses. The stimulus that triggers this system is sensation (that is, the five senses). Your E score is in fact an estimate of the point at which your motoric nervous system is aroused and, in effect, shouts, "Enough stimulation. Let there be quiet and stillness! Away, now, let me be!" The afferent nerves become saturated with sensation and crave respite. People with higher E scores can take more sensation before becoming saturated, a "sock it to me!" outlook. Traditionally, Extraversion has been associated with sociability, the tendency to prefer the company of other people. We know now, however, that the underlying reason is the need for sensory stimulation, and other people are the most common source of such stimulation. Yes, we can certainly feel in the thick of things if we are alone in a robotic manufacturing facility full of intense noises, sights, and smells, but if we are on the floor of a convention exhibition with fifty exhibitors and ten thousand conventioneers, ah, then we really *are* in the thick of things.

Let's now take a closer look at the types of behavior associated with the three areas of the E dimension.

Introvert (E–)

If you are an Introvert, you tend to prefer working alone and, if possible, will gravitate toward projects where you can work by yourself or with as few people as possible. Typically, you're a serious, quiet, private person who may prefer writing or e-mail to talking with co-workers. To others, you may come across as cold, hard to read, or reclusive. You may also appear to be a loner or even an eccentric to others. Your preferred work environment is in an area where you experience very little sensory stimulation. The "roar of the crowd, the smell of the greasepaint" doesn't appeal to you. You would much prefer to be "far from the madding crowd"!

Ambivert (E=)

If you are an Ambivert, you tend to move easily from working with other people to working alone. If you have to be in an environment with people all the time or work exclusively alone, you will probably find either extreme dissatisfying. Although you have a moderate threshold for sensory stimulation, you usually get tired of it after a while and try to get away from it. You may come across as an Introvert if your co-workers are strong Extraverts or as an Extravert if they are strong Introverts, because you operate from the midrange. Other Ambiverts will find you similar to themselves, sometimes wanting to be with others, sometimes wanting to be alone.

Extravert (E+)

If you are an Extravert, you tend to prefer being around other people and in the thick of the action. Your natural style is to be talkative, enthusiastic, sociable, warm, and fun-loving. It's highly likely that you will be comfortable with strong sensory stimulation—loud sounds such as music or crowd noise, sights such as bright lights, tastes such as those you might encounter during an elegant meal, smells such as those coming from vendors' carts on a city street, or touch as in the rush of wind past your face when you are skiing. You often become the formal or informal leader of your work team. However, you may at times come across to others as

E
Extraversion
WorkPlace Big Five ProFile

E1: Enthusiasm: How much we express positive feelings to others

E1– (Low)	Holds down positive feelings
E1= (Medium)	Demonstrates some positive feelings
E1+ (High)	Shows a lot of positive feelings

E2: Sociability: The degree to which we enjoy being with others

E2– (Low)	Prefers working alone
E2= (Medium)	Occasionally seeks out others
E2+ (High)	Prefers working with others

E3: Energy mode: Our need for keeping on the move

E3– (Low)	Prefers being still or in one place
E3= (Medium)	Maintains a moderate activity level
E3+ (High)	Prefers to be physically active

E4: Taking charge: The extent to which we want to lead others

E4– (Low)	Prefers being independent of others
E4= (Medium)	Accepts some responsibility for others
E4+ (High)	Enjoys the responsibility of leading others

E5: Trust of others: How easily we believe other people

E5– (Low)	Is skeptical of others
E5= (Medium)	Is somewhat trusting of others
E5+ (High)	Readily trusts others

E6: Tact: The degree of care we take in speaking

E6– (Low)	Speaks without special regard for consequences
E6= (Medium)	Exerts moderate care in selecting words for a particular situation
E6+ (High)	Carefully selects the appropriate words

Extraversion
NEO PI-R

E1: *Warmth: Our capacity for affection; friendliness; cordiality*

E1– (Low)	Is reserved, formal
E1= (Medium)	Is engaging without enthusiasm
E1+ (High)	Is affectionate, friendly, intimate

E2: *Gregariousness: Our preference for being around other people*

E2 (Low)	Seldom seeks company
E2= (Medium)	Mixes well, but enjoys privacy
E2+ (High)	Is gregarious, prefers company

E3: *Assertiveness: Our tendency to express ourselves forcefully and without reluctance*

E3– (Low)	Keeps opinions to self
E3= (Medium)	Expresses opinions as needed
E3+ (High)	Is assertive, speaks up, leads

E4: *Activity: Level of energy; our tendency toward a fast-paced lifestyle*

E4– (Low)	Has a leisurely pace
E4= (Medium)	Has an ordinary pace and energy level
E4+ (High)	Has a vigorous pace

E5: *Excitement seeking: Our appetite for the thrills of bright colors and noisy settings*

E5– (Low)	Has a low need for thrills
E5= (Medium)	Enjoys sensory stimulation
E5+ (High)	Craves intense excitement

E6: *Positive emotions: Our capacity for laughter, joy, love, optimism, and happiness*

E6– (Low)	Is less exuberant
E6= (Medium)	Has tempered optimism
E6+ (High)	Is cheerful, optimistic

outspoken, overbearing, aggressive, heedless, or shallow. You may also lack good listening skills because of your tendency to dominate a conversation.

The E Facets with Definitions

We have identified six important facets of Extraversion for the workplace and included them in the WorkPlace Big Five ProFile. Their definitions are given on page 58, along with anchors (descriptive phrases) for the high, midrange, and low ranges of each facet's continuum. The first three facets have parallel facets on the NEO, while the fourth, "taking charge," does not. "Excitement seeking" and "positive emotions," the fifth and sixth facets of the NEO, have no parallel in the WorkPlace version. The facets of the NEO Extraversion factor are listed on page 59.

E Case Study 1
The Football Game

We two authors both score as Ambiverts. Our favorite Ambivert story relates to the first year that the Carolina Panthers played NFL football in Charlotte. In the interest of rallying around the home team and being supportive of this new NFL team in the Carolinas, we had bought tickets with some friends to a home game with the San Francisco Forty-Niners. On game day, after discovering the wonders of tailgating, we headed for Ericsson Stadium with the rest of the crowd.

As we made our way among the noisy throng to our seats, we found ourselves only four rows away from the playing field, seated behind some "TV-wannabe" folks who had come with large prepared signs and much enthusiasm. The game finally began, and within a short time, the Panthers were winning—a pleasant turn of events! During the first half, we were totally involved in the game and in conversations with our friends. When we scored, we sang the Panther fight song and enjoyed "high fives" with the enthusiasts sitting in front of us during the final high note of the song. By the time the game moved into the third quarter, the overly warm September sun was becoming unpleasant. With growing concern for our long-term hearing, we noticed that the volume of the stadium music was increasing several decibels with every new song played over the public address system. Even though the Panthers were still winning, the game had begun to drag by for us, and we longed for the end. When at last the final minutes ticked off the game clock, we cheered our victory and made our way out of the stadium with the whooping fans.

At the front gate, one of our more extraverted friends said, "Hey, there are parties with live bands downtown. Let's head there for the celebration!" Our eyes met in silent, pleading assent, signaling escape. We politely declined the offer and told our friends that we would just walk home, since we lived near the stadium and were ready for some exercise. Although we had enjoyed the earlier part of the outing, by the time the game was over, we'd had enough—enough of the crowd, enough of the loud music, enough of the sensory bombardment. We had reached our Extraversion saturation point and were ready to introvert for the remainder of the day. Quietly, we walked home.

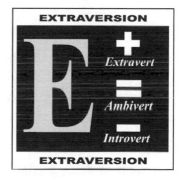

We like to use the expression "buckets": for each dimension, two buckets represent the amount of energy an individual has for each end of the continuum. Some people have a large bucket for crowds, a small bucket for solitude. They were the ones who went dancing after the game because they hadn't used up their bucket of "crowd fuel" yet! The people who have a small bucket for crowds and a large bucket for solitude stayed home and watched the game on television, with the sound turned down, if not off. We, as Ambiverts, have roughly equal-sized buckets for crowds and solitude, and we eventually ran out of crowd fuel—we were running on fumes and desperately needed to switch to our solitude bucket.

E Case Study 2

Reviewing the Memo

In the workplace, we have often observed that Extraverts tend to enjoy popping into a co-worker's office or cubicle in a situation such as this:

E+ (Extravert): "Hi, Fred! You look like you're really into that report you're typing."

E– (Introvert, flatly): "I was."

E+: "Well, since you've stopped, take a look at this memo for me, will you?"

E–: "OK, leave it and I will."

E+: "I was hoping you could just look it over and give me your thoughts. I really want to send it out within the next few minutes."

E– (sighing audibly): "I really prefer having time to read and digest it first."

E+: "I'm not looking for a three-hour speech from you about it. I simply want to hear off the top of your head if you think the memo covers the major points from our meeting last week."

E–: "Take it to Jill. She's better with fast responses than I am. Otherwise, I need until tomorrow to look it over."

E= (Ambivert, walking by):	"What are you guys up to?"
E+:	"I need a quick critique of this memo. I want to send it out right away, and Fred says he needs until tomorrow to 'read and digest' what I've written before he answers. He suggested you might do it faster."
E=:	"Well, I agree with Fred. You don't always give us time to look at something before you want to talk about it. You've waited four days since the meeting to send it out, a few more minutes won't make any difference. Give me the memo and show up at my desk in an hour. I'll give you my comments then so you can e-mail the memo today."
E+:	"Great!"

Situations like this happen constantly in the workplace when we don't understand the personalities of our co-workers. Without knowing how others handle or process information, we often assume that it's the same way we do. When they try to tell us differently, we may incorrectly assume that they're just being uncooperative, they don't care about our project, or even that they don't like us.

E Case Study 3
The Recognition Event

"You have just been told that your organization wants to honor you. Expense is no object. The size of the event, who will be invited, the location of the event, and the way you'll be honored are entirely up to you." When they were given this situation, fifty leaders responded in these ways:

E−− (extreme Introverts):	"I'd like a manager I respect to call me on the phone or e-mail me and tell me that I'm doing a good job."
E− (moderate Introverts):	"I'd like a dinner for my spouse and me at a nice restaurant. It would be quiet and dark and there'd be a fire in the restaurant fireplace."
E= (Ambiverts):	"I'd like a gathering of my teammates where we could have a nice meal in an elegant setting. We would all wear evening dress and celebrate the work of the team. There wouldn't be any speeches, just a nice time knowing what we had accomplished."
E+ (moderate Extraverts):	"I'd want to get the whole department together with our families and have a picnic at the lake. There'd be boating, skiing, horseshoes, volleyball, games for the kids, and lots of good food and drinks. The department manager might give me a plaque for the accomplishment."
E++ (extreme Extraverts):	"I'd rent the local stadium and send invitations to everyone I know or have ever met. I'd encourage people to bring their friends so there'd be a huge party atmosphere. Bands would

be playing from the field while everyone partied. There'd be all kinds of food and drink. The party would start at noon and go on for twenty-four hours. About midnight, I'd go up on the stage and thank everyone for coming. Then the company president would tell everyone what I'd done. An annual scholarship would be set up in my honor, and all the broadcast media would cover the event and interview me. Afterward, we would take a two-week cruise with a thousand of our closest friends!"

Obviously, the last scenario is rather far-fetched for the real workplace. Unlimited budgets are never available for parties. Still, interesting truths do emerge from these scenarios. Can you spot those that relate to Extraversion?

One of the most obvious elements is the number of people who are involved in each scenario. As we move from E–– at the low end of the scale to E++ at the high end, the number of people who are included in the event increases, from one manager by telephone, to my spouse, to my team, to my department, to everyone I ever knew and their friends! One reason for this increase is that additional people contribute to the sensation of the overall experience. This relates to sociability, our second element of Extraversion. You will also notice that the examples tend to talk more and more about the senses as the E score increases—more sights, more sounds, more tastes, more sensations for the body to experience. A third element in analyzing the responses has to do with how large a leadership role the person is comfortable taking when being recognized.

IMPLICATIONS FOR YOUR JOB AND CAREER

If you are E–, you will want to select jobs, roles, tasks, and other assignments that provide you with the solitude and quiet that you prefer. Your strength is in your capacity to shine alone with minimal stimulation—that is, in doing outpost work. You can be around crowds for a little while, but you'll be eager to get away. Imagine the introverted plumber who loves fixing the plumbing in private homes—quiet, little activity, no or very few people around. One day, he's called upon to help fix the plumbing in a day care center, with two dozen toddlers beating pie pans unrhythmically and the poor E– plumber yearning for an empty house to plumb. His bucket for crowds would run dry in a matter of minutes!

If you are E+, your strength is in working where all the action is. You would be miserable with solitude and silence, instead yearning for, and finding, sources of sensory stimulation to make you feel alive.

If you are E=, then one of two patterns is true for you. You may prefer alternating episodes of crowds and solitude, as in working a trade show in the morning, then doing paperwork in the afternoon, or you may prefer not to have either crowds or solitude, choosing instead the moderate stimulation of a small group of people.

IMPLICATIONS FOR YOUR BOSS AND ASSOCIATES

If you are E– with an E+ boss or associates, be prepared to ask for what you need with respect to meetings and drop-in conferences. Let them know that you do better when meetings are briefer, when you have an agenda in advance, and when you've been warned beforehand if you personally need to address any items in the meeting; remind them that you like to organize your thoughts in writing before appearing in a meeting or other type of discussion. Be understanding and nonjudgmental of their comfort with casual and extended chat sessions, but be clear in letting your limits be known. They may take your desire for solitude personally, so reassure them that it's nothing personal, just a difference in style.

If you are E+ with an E– boss or associates, be aware that it's unnatural for them to be productive in the same way you are. You will likely get better input from them if you ask in advance, preferably in writing, giving them time to think about the topic, get organized, and put their ideas on paper before meeting you face-to-face.

If you and your boss or associates are all E–, be aware that you may tend to undercommunicate. Find a way to touch base with each other on a regular basis, whether through e-mail or face-to-face. If you and your boss or associates are all E+, be aware of a tendency to overcommunicate, to take too long in meetings, and to interrupt others when they are trying to concentrate.

Before beginning the next chapter, make sure that you have entered your best estimate of your E score on the pullout profile that is part of the back cover of this book.

Curiosity

Originality/Openness to Experience

66 *When I examine myself and my methods of thought, I come close to the conclusion that the gift of fantasy has meant more to me than my talent for absorbing positive knowledge.* 99

—Albert Einstein, in his eighties

66 *'Men of action,' whose minds are too busy with the day's work to see beyond it, . . . are essential men, we cannot do without them, and yet we must not allow all our vision to be bound by the limitations of 'men of action.'* 99

—Pearl S. Buck

66 *All history is but a romance, unless it is studied as an example.* 99

—George Croly

Nineteenth-century Irish journalist and hymn writer George Croly strikes a stark standard for how we think in the Preserver mode—no idle recall of the past, please, unless it has practical utility for the here and now. Albert Einstein, on the other extreme, affirms the leadership of fantasy in dealing with facts. The balanced, tempered position is elaborated by Pearl Buck, who speaks for the Moderate when she insists that there be a balance between "action" and "vision." These are the central issues that comprise the O (Originality, or Openness) dimension.

The Biological Basis for Curiosity

The arousal system that provides the basis for the O set of behaviors is a combination of the dopaminergic system and the general state of arousal of the cerebral cortex. Dopamine is proving to be the "creativity" chemical, with levels of dopamine and dopamine receptors related to one's capacity to hold visual images in one's mind, whether they are visionary, futuristic images or hallucinations. The stimulus that triggers this system's switch from curiosity seeking back to familiar territory is novelty—that is, anything unfamiliar, whether it's in the form of ideas, foods, theories, values, art, skills, hobbies, or words. Your O score, then, is an estimate of when you've used up your available dopamine in your pursuit of novelty and your system says, "Whoa! No more novelty or complexity. Take me back to the simple and familiar, the tried and true."

Let's now take a closer look at the types of behavior associated with the three areas of the O dimension.

Preserver (O–)

If you are a Preserver, you tend to possess expert knowledge about a particular interest, topic, or subject. You're practical and down-to-earth, with a here-and-now view of the world. Your approach to work is efficient and you're comfortable with repetitive kinds of activity in your job. At times, others may view you as conservative, too narrow in your thinking, set in your ways, or rigid. You may prefer tried-and-true experiences or traditional ways of doing things.

Moderate (O=)

If you are a Moderate, you tend to be middle-of-the-road and somewhat down-to-earth, but you'll consider a new way of doing something if convincing evidence is available. Although you aren't known for your creativity or curiosity, these qualities will occasionally surface. At times, you may adopt a good idea from someone else and then develop it. You appreciate both innovation and efficiency, but you may not be able to do either one as naturally as people with higher or lower scores than yours.

Explorer (O+)

If you are an Explorer, you tend to have many broad interests and like to be on the cutting edge of new technology and Ideas. You are often curious, introspective, and reflective, seeking new and varied experiences and thinking about the future. However, you may become easily bored. In your view, you're probably quite liberal and feel comfortable with theory and concepts. You would describe yourself as creative, imaginative, or artistic, although others may believe that you're living in a fantasy world, are impractical, or are not in touch with day-to-day, here-and-now reality.

The O Facets with Definitions

We have identified four important facets of Originality, or Openness to Experience, for the workplace and included them in the WorkPlace Big Five ProFile. Their definitions follow on page 72, along with anchors (descriptive phrases) for the high, mid-range, and low ranges of each facet's continuum. The NEO PI-R has six facets of the Big Five for us to consider for both work and play. Three of these facets have no parallel in the WorkPlace version: aesthetics, feelings, and values. The NEO's O facets are listed on page 73.

O Originality
WorkPlace Big Five ProFile

O1:   *Imagination: Our preference for inventing plans and ideas*

O1– (Low)	Implements plans
O1= (Medium)	Creates and implements equally
O1+ (High)	Creates new plans and ideas

O2:   *Complexity: The extent to which we make things complex*

O2– (Low)	Prefers simplicity
O2= (Medium)	Prefers a balance of simplicity and complexity
O2+ (High)	Seeks complexity

O3:   *Change: How easily we accept change*

O3– (Low)	Wants to maintain existing methods
O3= (Medium)	Is somewhat accepting of changes
O3+ (High)	Readily accepts changes and innovations

O4:   *Scope: Our tolerance for handling details*

O4– (Low)	Is attentive to details
O4= (Medium)	Attends to details if needed
O4+ (High)	Prefers a broad view and resists details

Openness to Experience
NEO PI-R

O1: Fantasy: Creation of an interesting inner world through imagination and fantasy

O1– (Low)	Focuses on the here and now
O1= (Medium)	Has a limited fantasy life
O1+ (High)	Is imaginative, daydreams

O2: Aesthetics: A wide and deep appreciation for the arts and beauty; sensitivity

O2– (Low)	Is uninterested in art
O2= (Medium)	Has a sparing interest in art
O2+ (High)	Has an appreciation of art and beauty

O3: Feelings: The ability to value and experience a wide range of positive and negative emotions for ourselves and others

O3– (Low)	Ignores or discounts feelings
O3= (Medium)	Is accepting of feelings
O3+ (High)	Values all emotions

O4: Actions: A preference for novelty and variety over the routine and familiar

O4– (Low)	Prefers the familiar
O4= (Medium)	Likes a mixture of new and old
O4+ (High)	Prefers variety, tries new things

O5: Ideas: Intellectual curiosity; openness to new and unconventional ideas

O5– (Low)	Has a narrower intellectual focus
O5= (Medium)	Has a judicious interest in new ideas
O5+ (High)	Has a broad intellectual curiosity

O6: Values: Willingness to examine social, political, and religious values; a nondogmatic attitude

O6– (Low)	Is dogmatic, conservative
O6= (Medium)	Is middle-of-the-road
O6+ (High)	Is open to reexamining values

O Case Study 1

Management Trio Meets New Software

Let's listen in as three managers from the low, medium, and high ranges of the O scale converse:

O+ *(Explorer):*	"What a trade show I just attended! It's amazing what great new technology is out there!"
O– *(Preserver):*	"So that's where you were for the last 2½ days. I've been wanting to see you to go over some details in your last expense account submission. There are some significant errors in your math."
O+:	"Well, those can wait. I just don't have time to get bogged down in all those itty-bitty facts."
O= *(Moderate):*	"Yeah, but if you don't do at least some of the details, ol' Jill [O–] will find ways to keep from reimbursing you!"
O–:	"Well, I think you both like getting your yearly bonuses because someone like me concentrates on efficiencies and details around here."
O=:	"You've certainly got that right!"
O+:	"Well, you guys aren't going to believe what I saw at the trade show. I saw the next generation of software technology we have to buy! It's going to put our company way out in front of our competition. When we get the new software installed, we'll be offering our customers services we never dreamed about before. It'll revolutionize the way we do business and those bonuses will skyrocket next year. Our president is going to love it!"

O–:   "Oh yeah? The software we have now is perfectly good. I don't think anyone wants to go through the pain of changing over again after what we experienced two years ago. That software conversion was enough change to last a lifetime. Besides, just where do you think you're going to get the money to purchase this new software?"

O+:   "We always find the money if it's good for business. You've got to change to stay ahead of the competition. Look what happened to that company over in Columbus. They didn't convert to the new software like we did, and they lost out to us on that contract with ACME last year."

O–:   "They lost out because they didn't pay enough attention to their bottom line. They were financially unstable and ACME knew it."

O=:   "I really don't think ACME had a clue about their bottom line. I have a friend at ACME who told me that ACME awarded us the contract because of what our company could offer in the way of upgraded services, and that new software made this all possible. You know, as much as I hate to say it, Isabelle [O+] may have a point. It's been two years since we upgraded the software. In this day and age, if we don't continually upgrade, we could get left in the dust by our competition. We can't be complacent. Maybe we don't need to convert to the new technology this week, but we better start planning now to get it into next year's budget. As much as I hate to admit it, Isabelle has an uncanny way of anticipating new marketplace trends!"

As our case study shows, the O scale can contribute to conflict within the workplace when an O+ brings in new ideas or new ways of doing work. Usually the O– will resist this new idea or way of working, preferring to stick to well-proven historical methods, especially if the methods are cost-effective and are working well. Typically, the O= can begin to perceive some value in the O+'s new ideas but may wish to temper these ideas somewhat for the day-to-day reality of the workplace.

O Case Study 2
Making Sense of Scents

When we distribute a brightly colored scented marker, then ask people to thoroughly describe the object before time is called, we usually get the following responses:

O–– (extreme Preserver):
"It's a 5-inch cylinder, ¾-inch round base, red, shiny hard plastic [plus actual words copied from the marker, such as "Made by . . . ," "Do not shake," and "© date"], sixteen smiley faces with fruit shapes, white base, eight ridges inside the base."

O– (mild Preserver):
"It's a 5-inch cylinder, ¾-inch round base, red, shiny plastic, smiling faces of fruit, "Do not shake," white base with ridges, take off the cap, look, the cap fits in the base, chiseled point on writing tip, smells like cherry."

O= (Moderate):
"It's 5 inches long, little round base, it's kind of a cherry-colored red, shiny outside, take off the cap, listen, it makes a nice popping sound when you take off the cap, it writes red on flipcharts."

O+ (mild Explorer):
"It's cherry-colored, about 6 inches long, it's shiny and glistening, take off

the cap, hey, that's a good sound, umm—smells good, kids could use it for a clicker, you can draw fat and skinny lines with it, hey look, it rolls like a rolling pin, teachers can use these to liven up classrooms, kids would love to color with these things."

O++ (extreme Explorer):

"It's bright, smooth, take off the cap, it's a pretty color to look at, it's kind of pointy on the end. [What are you doing?] I'm tasting it to see if it tastes like cherry, yuck! They definitely didn't pick this cherry off the tree, the cap looks like a crown, or a space capsule zooming around the Earth, you could connect a bunch of these together to make a colorful pointer, you could stand ten of them up like bowling pins and then bowl them down, we could paint our fingernails with it."

Notice that you hear more specific details about the marker from the lower-scoring groups and that the higher-scoring groups basically ignore the details as they come up with their zany ideas.

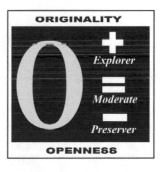

In a team within a manufacturing company, one very low-scoring group insisted that the high-scoring group didn't follow the directions! What emerged from the discussion was that O– people tended to stick with the object, focusing in on it, whereas O+ people tended to view the object in a much larger context and look at its possibilities; O= people did some of both with the object. This discussion led to a new appreciation for what different people on the team brought to their manufacturing workplace.

As it turned out, the O– people were content doing repetitive manufacturing jobs and concentrating on doing each task the same way every time, thereby guaranteeing high quality from the production line. The company valued this consistency. The O+ people, on the other hand, were not content with constant repetition. They became bored and started to look for new and possibly improved ways of doing the task. Some of their creative ideas and experiments were not as high-quality as the proven methods, but if they developed a better way of doing the same task, it sometimes became a new, cost-effective technique that was adopted by the O– and O= people.

O Case Study 3
Choosing a Leasing Agent

Suppose that you are the leasing division manager for a large real estate company and that you score in the middle range on the Openness scale with a score of 53. One important responsibility of your job is to hire and manage people who are the leasing agents for each of the eleven apartment properties that you supervise.

Throughout your seven years as the manager of this division, you've been reasonably successful in locating leasing agents who've been able to keep these existing apartment properties between 93 and 97 percent occupancy, percentages that are considered to be outstanding in your company and your industry. You're good at hiring and managing these leasing agents, whose jobs are quite repetitious. Basically, they meet walk-in prospects for apartments, complete paperwork, show apartments, and prepare reports. They have predictable budgets for brochures and a few novelty items with the apartment name and logo that they give to new residents once they've signed the lease. Occasionally, you may be called upon to help with a few promotional ideas when the leasing rate falls below 93 percent, but usually the leasing agents can do their jobs without much assistance from you. On the Big Five, these agents' O scores seem to cluster around 38.

Recently, your company built a new residential property, its first new one in nine years. Rather than inheriting already well-leased apartment buildings as you did upon assuming this job, you find yourself with 250 unoccupied apartment units to fill. The question facing you is this: Do you move your most dependable leasing agent to this new property from one of your other existing properties, or should you hire someone else with a different personality to take on this new responsibility?

Although it might be more comfortable for you to move one of your existing leasing agents into the new property, the results might not be what you'd expect. Our experience with clients in the real estate field indicates that the people who lease new properties need to be different from those who keep existing properties at capacity. In order to lease 250 apartments, the leasing agent probably needs to be very creative. O+ people tend to have the ideas that are necessary to get the apartments leased rapidly and are usually able to develop novel and clever marketing campaigns. Although they'll probably spend more money to lease each apartment than your other leasing agents do, these are the people you need in place during a start-up situation. In fact, in the real estate industry, they are known as preleasing specialists, whereas people who keep existing properties at capacity are known as leasing agents. This new position calls for a preleasing specialist with an O+ score of about 60 or above. Then, once the apartment complex is fully leased, bring in one of your consistent O– leasing agents to maintain the property and keep it at capacity.

IMPLICATIONS FOR YOUR JOB AND CAREER

If you are O–, you tend to take pride in tasks that require efficiency, precision, and thorough attention to detail. For you, repetition provides the opportunity to increase performance quality, as in "practice makes perfect." Use your comfort with routine to your advantage in jobs and tasks that require a no-nonsense approach to high production and demanding quality standards. Avoid roles that require you to deal with uncertainty, ambiguity, lack of structure, and figuring out the future for prolonged periods. You're a practical, here-and-now, get-the-work-out-the-door kind of worker. If you're a trainer, you're able to teach the same training seminar week after week, taking pleasure in continuing to polish your performance.

If you are O+, you need to avoid jobs or roles that require repetition, because you easily become bored doing the same thing more than once. You require a job with great latitude or job autonomy so that you can play what-if scenarios in your head, try to imagine what tomorrow will bring, and create new products and services for both new and old markets.

If you are O=, one of two situations will be more likely to satisfy you: either a balance of two extreme types of activity or more moderate activity that doesn't become extreme in either direction. On one hand, you may like an alternation between more creative tasks and more repetitive tasks, as in big-picture conversations (O+) in a morning meeting followed by proofreading (O–) in the afternoon. On the other hand, you may prefer activities throughout the day that are neither particularly creative (O+) nor particularly repetitive (O–), such as writing memos or handling customer service issues.

 IMPLICATIONS FOR YOUR BOSS AND ASSOCIATES

If you are O– and your boss or associates are O+, build on your value to them as a producer. They don't care about implementing plans and taking care of the details; instead, they would rather dream things up and solve problems. You will endear yourself to them by taking what they see as the drudgery of their work away from them, while they can take away the side that's frustrating for you—the cerebral, vague, what-if game of scenario planning.

If you are O+ and your boss or associates are O–, realize that they may tire of your suggestions and prefer that you put more effort into production. If you thrust your ideas on them too frequently, they'll begin to see you as a dreamer, a spender—as overhead rather than profit. Be selective in your imaginative initiatives. Pick your visionary battles!

Before beginning the next chapter, make sure that you have entered your best estimate of your O score on the pullout profile that is part of the back cover of this book.

Negotiation

5

Accommodation/ Agreeableness

+

  As thou wilt; what thou wilt; when thou wilt.

—Thomas à Kempis

=

  The generous who is always just, and the just who is always generous, may, unannounced, approach the throne of heaven.

—Johann Kaspar Lavater

–

  I believe in the brotherhood of man, all men, but I don't believe in brotherhood with anybody who doesn't want brotherhood with me. I believe in treating people right, but I'm not going to waste my time trying to treat somebody right who doesn't know how to return that treatment.

—Malcolm X

Thomas à Kempis expresses the highly agreeable, or accommodating, attitude that is characterized by subordinating one's will to that of someone else. It is reminiscent of the attitude of Ruth in the Old Testament ("Whither thou goest, I will go"), of Nora in Ibsen's *A Doll's House* ("I have been your doll wife"), and of the New Testament concept of "turn the other cheek." Malcolm X stakes out the other extreme, more reflective of the Old Testament view of "an eye for an eye and a tooth for a tooth." In fact, by the end of *A Doll's House,* Nora realizes that she must draw upon her A– resources when she musters the courage to tell her husband, Torvald, "I must learn to stand alone. That's why I can't stay here with you any more. . . . I have another duty equally sacred. . . . My duty to myself," as she slams the door on the repression of women. The third point of view, that of Lavater, urges the more balanced view, suggesting that there may be virtue in justice tempered with generosity.

The Biological Basis for Negotiation

The arousal system that governs the A set of behaviors consists of the sex hormones, along with the serotonergic system. The stimulus that triggers this system into action is the dominance challenge. For people with a relative abundance of the male hormones, such as testosterone, and a relative deficit of the female hormones, such as estrogen and progesterone, defiance is the norm. As the balance of sex hormones shifts, whether in males or females, the norm shifts from defiance to submission. Your A score, then, is an estimate of the point at which you tire of being defiant and turn to acts of submission. Serotonin levels affect this trigger point: higher levels are associated with relaxation and peacefulness, lower levels with aggression (and, in some conditions, depression).

Let's now take a closer look at the types of behavior associated with the three areas of the A dimension.

Challenger (A–)

If you are a Challenger, you tend to relate to authority by being skeptical, tough, guarded, persistent, competitive, or aggressive. Often, you are independent in your thoughts and ask questions, especially to protect your self-interest and to make sure you win. At times you may come across to others as hostile, rude, aloof, self-centered, proud, haughty, hard-headed, or combative.

Negotiator (A=)

If you are a Negotiator, you tend to be able to shift between competitive and cooperative situations fairly easily, usually pushing for a win-win strategy. You probably have a comfortable sense of personal identity, neither excessively dependent nor excessively independent. Typically, you can work well either as a team member or as an independent. At your worst moments, you might be regarded by others as sitting on the fence between opposite views as you try to help both sides to compromise.

Adapter (A+)

If you are an Adapter, you tend to relate to authority by being tolerant, humble, and accepting. Often, you defer to other people and are seen as helpful, easily moved, and a team player. Typically, you may allow others to win or be right more than you allow yourself to. At times, you may come across to others as spineless, naive, submissive, conflict-averse, gullible, dependent, or even unprincipled (because you keep yielding your position).

The A Facets with Definitions

We have identified five important facets of Accommodation, or Agreeableness, for the workplace and included them in the WorkPlace Big Five ProFile. Their definitions are given on page 84, along with anchors (descriptive phrases) for the high, midrange, and low ranges of each facet's continuum. All five of the workplace facets have direct parallels in the NEO PI-R model: service mode equals altruism, agreement equals compliance, and so forth. Two of the WorkPlace facets—reserve and reticence—are included elsewhere on the NEO model—reserve is assertiveness (E3) on the NEO, and reticence is self-consciousness (N4) on the NEO. In the workplace, these two facets are correlated more strongly with the A factor than with their NEO factors (N and E). On the other hand, two

A

Accommodation
WorkPlace Big Five ProFile

A1: *Service: How readily we inconvenience ourselves for others*

A1– (Low)	Is more interested in self needs
A1= (Medium)	Is interested in the needs of others and self
A1+ (High)	Is more interested in others' needs

A2: *Agreement: Our driving force during conflict*

A2– (Low)	Welcomes engagement
A2= (Medium)	Seeks resolution
A2+ (High)	Seeks harmony

A3: *Deference: Our desired level of recognition*

A3– (Low)	Wants acknowledgment
A3= (Medium)	Likes some acknowledgment
A3+ (High)	Is uncomfortable with acknowledgment

A4: *Reserve: The degree to which we voice our opinions to others*

A4– (Low)	Usually expresses opinions
A4= (Medium)	Expresses opinions somewhat
A4+ (High)	Keeps opinions to self

A5: *Reticence: How we feel in front of others*

A5– (Low)	Enjoys being out front
A5= (Medium)	Wants some visibility
A5+ (High)	Prefers the background

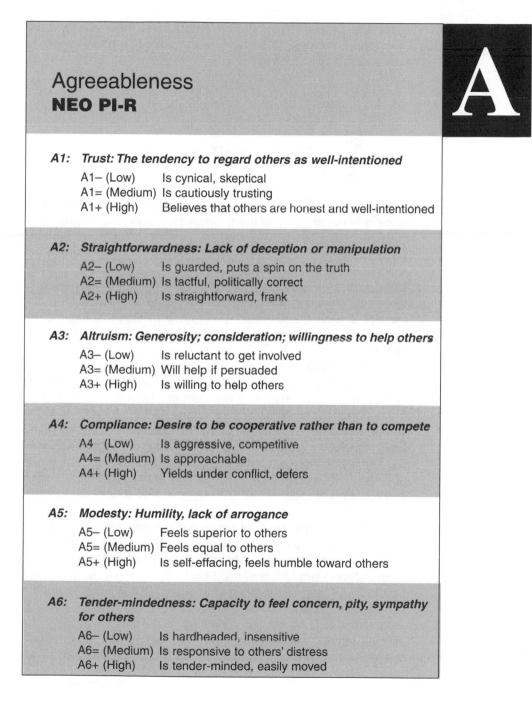

Agreeableness
NEO PI-R

A1: *Trust: The tendency to regard others as well-intentioned*

    A1– (Low)   Is cynical, skeptical
    A1= (Medium) Is cautiously trusting
    A1+ (High)   Believes that others are honest and well-intentioned

A2: *Straightforwardness: Lack of deception or manipulation*

    A2– (Low)   Is guarded, puts a spin on the truth
    A2= (Medium) Is tactful, politically correct
    A2+ (High)   Is straightforward, frank

A3: *Altruism: Generosity; consideration; willingness to help others*

    A3– (Low)   Is reluctant to get involved
    A3= (Medium) Will help if persuaded
    A3+ (High)   Is willing to help others

A4: *Compliance: Desire to be cooperative rather than to compete*

    A4 (Low)   Is aggressive, competitive
    A4= (Medium) Is approachable
    A4+ (High)   Yields under conflict, defers

A5: *Modesty: Humility, lack of arrogance*

    A5– (Low)   Feels superior to others
    A5= (Medium) Feels equal to others
    A5+ (High)   Is self-effacing, feels humble toward others

A6: *Tender-mindedness: Capacity to feel concern, pity, sympathy for others*

    A6– (Low)   Is hardheaded, insensitive
    A6= (Medium) Is responsive to others' distress
    A6+ (High)   Is tender-minded, easily moved

of the NEO A facets—trust and straightforwardness—load more heavily on the E factor, and so have been moved to the E factor as "trust of others" and "tact."

A Case Study 1

The Collections Team

Smaller consulting companies often will hire other consultants to help them when they land a large project. A consulting company that occasionally hired us for larger projects invited us in to use the Big Five with a newly formed team in the collections department of a food distribution company. Without knowing the personalities of the people on the team ahead of time, the consulting company had agreed to go into the food distribution company and set up the team, providing training in communication skills, leading meetings, problem-solving skills, and so forth.

The consulting company had held an initial session with the team to tell them about the project. Meanwhile, we had seen the scores of the team members we were to work with and asked for a meeting with the consulting company and the food distribution company manager before leading the session. At the meeting, realizing that we were probably terminating any future work with the consulting company, we announced that the current group of people who'd been assigned to this team probably wouldn't make it as a traditional team in spite of any training that might be provided.

The primary reason for our statement was that out of fifteen people assigned to the team, twelve scored in the A– area of the scale and three scored A=. In other words, these twelve people were independent and preferred to do their work their own way. Sharing work and cooperating in all areas of their jobs, which the consulting company had set as goals for the team, were unrealistic outcomes, given the personalities of the team members. As indicated by their scores, they were good at collecting from overdue accounts, primarily because they wouldn't take no as an answer. Their success had come from insisting that others comply with them. If it suited the situation, they could be rude or even harsh. They viewed the accounts they managed as their own personal accounts. Asking them to cooperate and share "their" accounts with other collectors was not the way to best use their strengths.

In spite of our recommendations and prognosis, the consulting company and food distribution company decided that they wanted to continue with the process of creating a cooperative, sharing team. Through later conversations with the food distribution company, we heard that over the next eighteen months, they had lost all twelve of the A– employees. Although they replaced them with other people who could function in a more cooperative and sharing environment, they lost a strong core of knowledge from their company and many years of experience. If they had redefined the purpose of the team and the way it would work, many of those people might have been retained without putting the company through the unnecessary, cumulative expense of hiring and training new employees.

A Case Study 2

A Vendor Reneges

We often ask team members how they would respond to this dilemma: "You're a member of a seven-member team that has been invited by one of your vendors to participate in a conference at a very posh resort. Unfortunately, one week before the conference, the vendor states that because of critical budget cuts, only five people from your seven-member team may now attend the conference. What will you do?" Here's how they usually respond:

A++ (extreme Adapters):	"We don't want to decide; just let management decide and tell us who's going." "I'd volunteer not to go because I've been to that resort

	before." "Let's just draw straws to see who goes." "We need to do something nice for the two people who have to stay behind."
A+ (moderate Adapters):	"Let's draw straws." "Which people need to go to the conference because of what they need to learn or present for the team?" "Should we look at some criteria for choosing who gets to go?"
A= (Negotiators):	"Let's draw straws." "What if we all chipped in our own money to make up the difference for the two people the vendor said can't go?" "We could do some fund-raising for our team so we can all go."
A– (moderate Challengers):	"Let's move the conference to a less expensive location so we can all go." "If the vendor promised, the vendor should take us." "Our organization can make up the budget difference for the other two people so they can go."
A–– (extreme Challengers):	"Well, I don't know about the rest of you, but I'm going!" "Tell the vendor we'll all go as promised, or we'll find a new vendor who'll take us." "It's too late to back out now; we're going and it's the vendor's problem to figure out how." "We're all going or nobody's going!"

People with a high score (A+) tend to accept the situation as it exists without question. They've been told that they may only take five of their seven members, and they accept that as unalterable fact. As we move down the scale to hear from other groups, there's a growing sense that we could (A=) and ultimately will (A–) do something differently. The A= group begins to negotiate other options, while the A-- group threatens to terminate the contract with the vendor unless the vendor makes good on the promised trip for seven people. A+ people will often give in for the good of the team; they are the ultimate team members. Conversely, A- people rarely can take a situation as it exists without asking questions or without some skepticism. A= people are capable of responding either way.

A Case Study 3
The Marketing Team at Work

To hear the A scale in action at work, let's listen in to the following conversation taking place during a three-person marketing team meeting (the facilitator of the meeting is the A= member):

A= (Negotiator): "Our next agenda item is what we should do about the problem of getting revised promotional material into the branch offices."

A+ (Adapter): "Well, since we're at headquarters, I think it's our responsibility to get the materials developed, printed, and shipped out to the branches. Those poor folks in the branches have their hands full just trying to deal with all the local walk-in business every day."

A- (Challenger): "What are you going to do about all the geographic differences? Just because the promotional material works in the eastern territory where we've pilot-tested it doesn't mean it will necessarily work in the western territory. I think the branches need the basic graphic design from us on disk so they can customize it for their markets with a local graphic designer. Then they can print the material locally and save the company all the shipping charges you want us to shell out with our budget."

A+:   "Oh, OK, I hadn't thought about that. We'll do it your way."

A–:   "There you go again—caving in to me without defending your idea. Stand up for yourself."

A+:   "I don't want to argue about it. We all need to get along to work together on this team. I'm fine doing it your way."

A=:   "Armando [A+], I think what Robin [A–] is trying to say is that she wants to discuss the agenda item further by asking some tough questions. And Robin, I think that Armando is trying to get the matter settled without any disagreement between us, because that makes him uncomfortable."

A+:   "That's true, and I know how pushed for time those people in the branches are."

A–:   "OK. What if we look for a way to customize the material for them, send it out to the regional branches for approval, get the printing done here in a large enough quantity to give us a good printing price, and charge the shipping back to their budgets instead of ours?"

A=:   "That sounds like a plan. Armando, what if you talk with the branches about their customization needs? You have great relationships with all those branch managers."

A+:   "Sure, I'd enjoy that."

A=:	"And Robin, what if you start negotiating a good quantity price for us with our printers?"
A–:	"OK. I think I can get them to cut the price by at least 5 percent over the last printing. But I want the branches to pay for the printing and shipping out of their budgets."
A=:	"We should be able to get them to agree to that since we handled it that way last year. Let's all bring our updates on this back to next week's meeting."

This script highlights some of the clear distinctions between the A– and A+ facets. The questioning that comes as second nature to an A– (Challenger) may be perceived as conflict to an A+ (Adapter). In order to preserve the "peace" of the team, the A+ selflessly yields his position for the "good" of the team. Meanwhile, the A– loses respect for him because she can't get a good argument from him. The A=, the facilitator in this case, becomes the translator between the A+ and A–. By explaining the needs and positions of the high and low scorers, the A= helps them to reach a compromise in which they both get their needs met and the team accomplishes its goal of providing revised materials to the branch offices.

IMPLICATIONS FOR YOUR JOB AND CAREER

If you are A–, your strength and your liability are one and the same: you question everything as a matter of course. Although this minimizes the possibility of groupthink, you continually risk resentment and alienation from others. Prefer a job that builds on such skepticism, such as accounting, engineering, or courtroom litigation.

If you are A+, again, your strength and your liability are identical: you tend to subordinate your needs to those of others as a matter of course. You will therefore always be valued as a team member, but you should be wary of situations in which you're responsible to someone with whom you don't share the same values, because you will find it next to impossible to stand up to that person when you need to.

If you are A=, you tend to be valued as a peacemaker and a negotiator, one who strives to achieve the win-win situation. Build on your natural ability to see both sides of a question.

 IMPLICATIONS FOR YOUR BOSS AND ASSOCIATES

If you are A– and your boss or associates are A+, be prepared to find little resistance to your thoughts, because they will probably tend to submit to your strong questioning and opinions. Be sure to take the time and effort to discover what they truly think; if you don't, they'll build up resentments over time and leave you. You may not respect their lack of "backbone," but trust that they really do have opinions, even if they don't have the courage to do battle with you.

If you are A+ and your boss or associates are A–, you're in danger of seldom getting your interests met unless you share the same values. Take the time and effort to put your thoughts and needs in writing, and use your notes as a form of muscle with which to approach them and stand up for your needs.

Before beginning the next chapter, make sure that you have entered your best estimate of your A score on the pullout profile that is part of the back cover of this book.

Focus

6

Consolidation/ Conscientiousness

The trouble with being number one in the world—at anything—is that it takes a certain mentality to attain that position in the first place, and that is something of a driving, perfectionist attitude, so that once you do achieve number one, you do not relax and enjoy it.

—Billie Jean King

All work and no play makes Jack a dull boy.

—James Howell

There is nothing insignificant.

—Samuel Taylor Coleridge

Tennis great Billie Jean King (holder of twenty Wimbledon titles) captures the essence of high C (Consolidation, or Conscientiousness) when she says that one should "not relax" in the pursuit of being "number one." That in a nutshell is the Focused personality trait. At the other extreme, the poet Coleridge expresses the lack of discipline and goal focus of the low C, the Flexible personality supertrait, when he speaks of nothing being "insignificant." By implication, when nothing is insignificant, no stone should be left unturned, every lead must be followed up, every idea must be chased—in short, it becomes impossible to focus or establish priorities. When everything is important, nothing is central. A character on the "Route 66" television program in the 1960s once commented about someone with a hippie lifestyle: "By loving everything, you end up truly loving nothing." Between these two extreme positions emerges the Balanced view, typified by seventeenth-century writer James Howell's call for play as well as work.

The Biological Basis for Focus

The arousal system that supports the C set of behaviors is the attentional focus system. This system is affected by levels of testosterone: higher levels are associated with a greater capacity to focus one's attention on sustained, repetitive, goal-focused behavior. Distractions are the stimuli that trigger the attentional system; they cause the individual to lose focus, or attention. Your C score, then, is an estimate of the point at which you finally say, "That's enough focusing for awhile. It's time to take a break, to play, to have a change of pace."

Let's now take a closer look at the types of behavior associated with the three areas of the C dimension.

Flexible (C–)

If you are a Flexible, you tend to approach goals in a relaxed, spontaneous, and open-ended fashion. Your mind is like a parallel processor, able to switch tracks on the run. You may be a procrastinator. You are able to multitask easily, becoming involved in many projects at the same time. However, you may be perceived as being casual about your responsibilities or as being unorganized, unproductive, or irresponsible. Marshall McLuhan once described people as varying on a scale from more goal-oriented to more role-oriented. The Flexible focuses more on the various roles played at work, while the Focused tends to focus on the overriding goal.

Balanced (C=)

If you are a Balanced, you tend to keep work demands and personal needs, goal demands and various roles, in good balance. Your mind operates at times like a parallel processor and at times like a serial processor, both switching tracks and proceeding linearly. You are probably more ambitious than a Flexible, yet more prone to enjoy leisure than a Focused. From time to time, you are able to interrupt your focus on goals with some spontaneous diversions.

Focused (C+)

If you are a Focused, you tend to work toward your goals in an industrious, disciplined, and dependable fashion. Your mind is like a serial processor, proceeding in a linear, sequential manner. You probably have a strong will to achieve and do so with hard work, good preparation, and much organization. When you promise to deliver, you do; your word is money in the bank. You typically consolidate your time, energy, and resources in pursuit of your goals. At times you may be perceived to be a workaholic, overly demanding, compulsive, meticulous, or stubborn.

The C Facets with Definitions

We have identified five important facets of Consolidation, or Conscientiousness, for the workplace and included them in the WorkPlace Big Five ProFile. Their definitions follow on page 96, along with anchors (descriptive phrases) for the high, midrange, and low ranges of each facet's continuum. Each of these facets has a direct parallel on the NEO PI-R: perfectionism equals competence, organization equals order, drive equals achievement striving, concentration equals self-discipline, and methodicalness

C

Consolidation
WorkPlace Big Five ProFile

C1:   *Perfectionism: The degree to which we strive for perfection*

C1– (Low)   Has a low need to continually refine or polish
C1= (Medium)   Has an occasional need to refine or polish
C1+ (High)   Has a continual need to refine or polish

C2:   *Organization: The degree to which we stay organized*

C2– (Low)   Is comfortable with little formal organization
C2= (Medium)   Maintains some organization
C2+ (High)   Keeps everything organized

C3:   *Drive: How pushed we feel to achieve*

C3– (Low)   Is satisfied with current level of achievement
C3= (Medium)   Needs some additional achievement
C3+ (High)   Craves even more achievement

C4:   *Concentration: How sustained our attention is*

C4– (Low)   Shifts easily between tasks
C4= (Medium)   Can shift between tasks before completion
C4+ (High)   Prefers to complete tasks before shifting to others

C5:   *Methodicalness: How much planning we need to do*

C5– (Low)   Operates in a more spontaneous mode
C5= (Medium)   Does some planning
C5+ (High)   Develops plans for everything

Consciousness
NEO PI-R

C

C1: *Competence: How prepared and capable we feel; level of self-esteem; possession of an Internal locus of control*

C1– (Low)   Often feels unprepared
C1= (Medium) Generally is prepared and confident
C1+ (High)   Feels capable and effective

C2: *Order: The tendency to be well-organized and methodical; neatness; the tendency to be compulsive*

C2– (Low)   Is unorganized, unmethodical
C2= (Medium) Is organized in some areas, but not in others
C2+ (High)   Is well-organized, neat, tidy

C3: *Dutifulness: Strict adherence to our conscience; reliability*

C3– (Low)   Is casual about obligations
C3= (Medium) Covers priorities, but can overcommit
C3+ (High)   Is guided by conscience, is reliable

C4: *Achievement striving: The tendency to set high goals and focus on them; the tendency toward workaholism*

C4– (Low)   Has a low need for achievement
C4= (Medium) Is serious about being successful
C4+ (High)   Is driven to achieve success

C5: *Self-discipline: The capacity to motivate ourselves to get the job done and resist distractions*

C5– (Low)   Procrastinates, is distracted
C5= (Medium) Is usually on-task, but can be distracted
C5+ (High)   Focuses on completing tasks

C6: *Deliberation: The ability to think something through before acting on it*

C6– (Low)   Is spontaneous, makes hasty decisions
C6= (Medium) Is sometimes thoughtful, sometimes spontaneous
C6+ (High)   Thinks carefully before acting

equals deliberation. The only facet on the NEO that doesn't have a parallel in the WorkPlace is dutifulness (C3 on the NEO). Certainly dutifulness is important in the workplace, so why did we omit it? First, it is highly correlated with Conscientiousness (.74), so that higher scores on C tend to be accompanied by higher scores on C3. Second, we have been unable to determine a positive attribute associated with low dutifulness, so including it would violate our principle of including only those traits that have positive features associated with both ends of the continuum. We will simply treat dutifulness, or reliability, doing what one says one will do, as an attribute of C+.

C Case Study 1
The Unscheduled Meeting

Do any of the following responses sound like you when a team member or co-worker asks you to join a spontaneous meeting that hasn't been scheduled in advance? For this case study, imagine that it's 8:50 A.M. and you're listening in as a team member visits the desks of three other team members who are all working on reports that are due by late afternoon. The requesting team member says, "I've just called a 9:00 meeting to discuss yesterday's production problem. Can you join us?" Here are the responses:

C– (Flexible):   "Sure. I'll grab my file and come right now."

C= (Balanced):   "Uh, OK. Give me about ten minutes to finish the first section in this report I'm writing, and I'll be there."

C+ (Focused):   "No, not right now. I'm in the middle of this report I have to finish this morning. I have an opening on my schedule at noon and could join you then."

All three people who were asked to join the meeting were working on reports due that afternoon, yet they responded in three distinct ways, depending upon their scores on the C scale.

People who are lower in C tend to be more spontaneous and manage multiple tasks during their day, although they sometimes lose track of their top priorities. People who score in the midrange stick to their tasks a little more easily but are still capable of being spontaneous. People who score in the high range stay with their goal or with the top priorities that will lead them to their goal, if at all possible. They prefer to finish what they're working on before starting another project. They also like to finish projects ahead of schedule.

C Case Study 2
The To-Do List

We sometimes ask people the following questions: "Think back over last weekend. Recall everything you planned to get done during the weekend. What percentage of what you planned to do did you accomplish? Did you add in extra items? Did you have a written list?" The answers typically are as follows:

C–– (extremely Flexible):

"Why should we have a plan for the weekend? We just let things happen." "I usually have a few things I want to get done going into the weekend. I feel pretty good if I get 20 to 25 percent of them done." "I have some things that I think about wanting to do for a long time before I finally get around to them, like painting the bathroom. I've been talking myself out of that one for about six months now."

C– (moderately Flexible):

"Going into the weekend, I usually know what I'm going to do and almost always add in some extra things." "I feel good if I get about half the things done that I want to get accomplished." "There are a couple of usual things I plan to do and know I'll get done, like buying groceries or getting my hair cut. But I like to be flexible to allow for anything unexpected that may come along." (About one out of five people will make a written list for the weekend, just to organize his or her thoughts, but may not follow it.)

C= (Balanced):

"Most of the time I get half to two-thirds of my list accomplished on the weekend." (About half of the small group will consistently have a written list. All of them will say that they have a mental list for the weekend.)

C+ (moderately Focused):

"I usually accomplish at least 80 to 90 percent of my list during the weekend." (Most of the group will use a written list and will admit to adding extra items to the list just for the joy of being able to cross them off afterward.)

C++ (extremely Focused):

"It's rare for me not to accomplish everything on my list for the weekend." (Most of these people say that they accomplish 100 to 120 percent of what they plan to do during the week-end, since a family member can usually get them to add in something extra.) "I often stay up later just to finish the items on my list before the workweek begins again." "If an item or an event isn't already on my to-do list or my schedule before the workweek ends, it won't be added once the weekend begins."

The important thing to remember is that the C– is not necessarily nonproductive in the workplace. Rather, people who score C– are just not as methodical as those who score C+. At times, C– people may actually accomplish more than C+ people, though in a less organized fashion. They also sometimes have to be reminded about the goal, since they may get sidetracked by the many tasks and responsibilities that compete for attention during the workday.

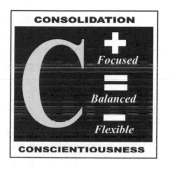

The C+, on the other hand, may get so focused on the goal and on staying with the assigned task that he or she may fail to flex around important new changes or immediate market conditions that need to be accommodated but that may not be stated in the organizational plan.

C Case Study 3
The Three Ministers

A large, well-run urban church has a team of three well-respected ministers comprised of two associate ministers and one senior minister. As you read about the ministers and their accompanying profiles, try to estimate where you think each minister scores on the C scale.

Minister 1: He is the senior minister of this congregation, a role that makes him, in effect, the chief executive officer of the church. In his position, he prepares and delivers most of the sermons and effectively oversees the day-to-day operations of the church and the staff of fourteen people. He is known as a good delegator. Still, even with his many responsibilities, he occasionally makes time to speak to or meet with members of his congregation who show up at his office door for a kind word or to discuss a problem. His sermons tend to keep the congregation alert because they're frequently based on well-researched, local social issues or interesting historical facts from a particular era.

Minister 2: He is the older associate minister and is in charge of pastoral care for the congregation. He's been in this field for thirty years. When someone in the congregation is sick, dies, or goes into the hospital, he visits the person or the family as soon as he hears of their difficulty. As a counselor, he's always available to any member who drops by the church or calls him at home needing to talk about a concern or a problem. His occasional sermons are not the best because he tends to ramble without making a clear point.

Minister 3: She is the younger associate minister and is in charge of the church's educational program. In this capacity, she develops and manages a very elaborate calendar of activities and a large cadre of volunteers. Her systematic file labels are color-coded, and she's known for allowing nothing to slip through the cracks. She sets attendance and participation goals and tracks them regularly. She rarely meets with members who just drop by; rather, she schedules them at a more convenient time. Her sermons follow a very systematic formula consisting of an introduction, three main points, and a closing. Most of the time, these sermons are rather predictable.

Now, you must decide. What C scores would you likely find for each of the three ministers?

If you assigned minister 1 the C=, you're correct. He is sometimes capable of being spontaneous and flexible with members who drop by, yet he can delegate well and seems to maintain a well-run organization without trying to do it all himself. Since he delivers most of the sermons, it appears that he's midrange on the C scale, finding time to prepare them while occasionally meeting with members who drop by his office.

If you placed minister 2 in the C− range, you're correct. His gift is in multitasking, whether he's visiting people who are sick or grieving or helping members with problems. When needed, he is there. Unfortunately, when his turn comes to prepare and deliver a sermon, he may not put quite as much time and effort into it as the other two ministers, since he's been busy responding to the other needs of the congregation's members.

If you said C+ for minister 3, you're correct. She is known and valued for her organizational skills, and she keeps the educational program going and growing, constantly setting new goals to achieve. However, the spontaneity of drop-by members is not something she handles well, scheduling them for times that better suit her schedule. And her well-organized, predictable sermons are, well, pretty much the same.

C IMPLICATIONS FOR YOUR JOB AND CAREER

If you are C–, you will likely find management responsibility an unnatural fit. You'll be frustrated by others' expectations that you be disciplined, focused, ambitious, and methodical when your true nature enjoys jumping from one task to another. Interruption is your middle name. Two pieces of advice: first, prefer staff to line positions. By staying away from management responsibility, you can emphasize your strength, which is jumping from the priorities of this moment to those of the next. Second, find jobs that have minimal job freedom or autonomy. Research (Bigazzi, Kello, and Marciano, 1999) has shown that people who are low in C achieve higher performance ratings in jobs with low freedom or autonomy, and lower performance ratings in jobs with a high degree of freedom, discretion, or autonomy. In other words, more highly constrained jobs give C– workers less opportunity to make counterproductive decisions, while highly autonomous jobs expose the weakness of C– workers—distractibility. Give them enough rope and they'll hang themselves.

If you are C+, your discipline, ambition, and focus will be sought after to perform management duties. If you choose to be entrepreneurial, your chances of success are high, because you possess the tenacity to both persevere until you've accomplished your goal and resist tempting distractions that can dilute and delay your efforts.

If you are C=, management is a viable option for you, but only in a nonworkaholic culture. In a workaholic setting, you'll feel pressured to put in the extra hours that violate your sense of balance between your personal and private lives.

IMPLICATIONS FOR YOUR BOSS AND ASSOCIATES

If you are C− and your boss or associates are C+, they represent a resource for keeping you organized and on schedule. Learn not to resent their focus and discipline, but rather to lean on it. For their part, they need to value your spontaneity and willingness to shift priorities in order to help them reach their goals. When you feel overwhelmed with multiple tasks, sit down with your C+ boss or associates and ask them to help you set priorities. And do it often, even daily!

If you are C+ and your boss or associates are C−, you're often going to feel like a stranger in a strange land. You and your boss may have your roles reversed—bosses are supposed to be disciplined, workers flexible. A boss who's low in C will need you to keep him or her and the office organized and focused. Offer your services; without them, your boss or associates will likely flounder, and you will look bad by association. Eventually, your contribution to team effectiveness will be rewarded. If you make it a competition in which you resist helping your boss or associates, you'll be regarded as a maverick who only looks out for number one and isn't a team player.

Before beginning the next chapter, make sure that you have entered your best estimate of your C score on the pullout profile that is part of the back cover of this book.

7

Traits

Working Together to Create Personality

We have now finished defining the five factors and the facets that comprise each of them. The remainder of this book focuses on how these traits relate to specific workplace behaviors. If you're champing at the bit to get into specific work applications, we can understand that you might want to skip this chapter and move on to the next part of the book. However, we think it would be wise to pause for a moment and review some of the ways that personality traits interact with each other and with issues other than personality traits. As Allport warned, personality traits don't exist in isolation, like a traffic light that changes inexorably from red to yellow to green to yellow and so on until it wears out or the power goes off. Unlike the venerable and reliable traffic light, human personality traits, though they do establish a pattern, are heavily characterized by exceptions to the rule. Just as all that glitters is not gold, all who chatter are not necessarily extraverted. Let's take a look at the many ways that traits behave.

Pures

We refer to the simplest level of trait behavior as "pures," short for "pure traits." A pure trait is a single factor or facet that expresses itself without the contribution of any other trait. Pures are uncomplicated and simple. A person who spends most of his or her time around other people would be said to be high in facet E2, sociability (or gregariousness). This would be an example of an E2 behaving in a pure manner.

E2 is a "primary" trait, in that it cannot be subdivided. Although different people might be sociable in different ways (for example, they may go to lots of meetings or trade shows, prefer open office spaces, or choose to work with a team), sociability *always* means a preference for being around other people. It may have different manifestations, but it always has the same underlying meaning.

Now let's make a wrinkle in this relatively straightforward concept. Each dimension (factor or facet) is defined by two opposing, or balancing, traits that anchor each end of the dimensional continuum. For example, E2 is defined at one end by *gregariousness* and at the other by *solitude*. In fact, these two anchors represent the two extremes of a particular quantity. E2+ represents a person with more desire for social contact and E2– represents one with less desire for social contact. Social contact is the quantity that is measured by E2, just as a thermometer measures temperature. Each of the factors and facets measures such a quantity in the same way. The more of the quantity there is, the less we demonstrate the behavior associated with its absence and the more we demonstrate the behavior associated with its presence. For example, the higher the E2 score, the less we demonstrate solitude and the more we demonstrate gregariousness. Conversely, the less of the quantity there is, the less we demonstrate the behavior associated with it and the more we demonstrate the behavior associated with its absence. For example, the lower the E2 score, the less we demonstrate gregariousness and the more we demonstrate solitude.

But what about midrange scores? If a person scores 50 on E2, just what does that mean? This is where trait theory gets a bit iffy. Follow this discussion by referring to Figure 7.1. There are two ways to get a midrange score of 50. On the one hand, an individual could answer half the questions about E2 with "Strongly agree" and the other half with "Strongly disagree." In this case, the individual implies a tendency to split time between the coliseum and the kitchen, between the discotheque and the den, or between the sales convention and the studio. In other words, this person would be a study in opposites, one balancing the other. This Ambivert gets his or her fill of large crowds and then retreats, only to become sated with solitude and return to the crowds. This would be reflected on a test as a midrange score of 50, halfway between 0 and 100. It would be the *average* of half lower scores and half higher scores, low scores representing solitude and high scores representing crowds.

On the other hand, an individual could answer all of the questions about E2 with midpoint, or "neutral," answers, never agreeing or disagreeing with questions about solitude or crowds. In this case, the individual expresses neither aversion to nor fondness for either end of the continuum. Rather, she or he is a study in moderation,

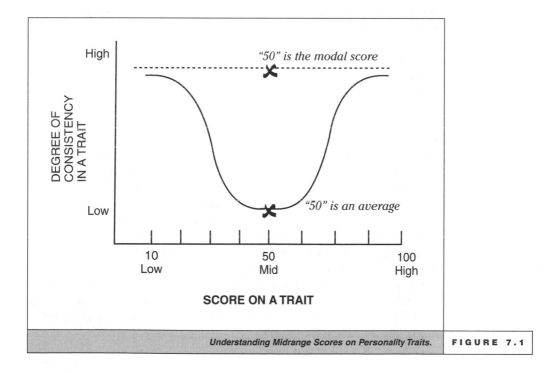

Understanding Midrange Scores on Personality Traits.   **FIGURE 7.1**

preferring manageable groups of people to either solitude or crowds. This Ambivert would tend to avoid both crowds and solitude, preferring family, friends, or co-workers in moderate numbers at all times. The score of 50 here wouldn't reflect an *average* of extreme scores; instead, it would reflect what statisticians call a *mode,* the score that occurs most frequently. In other words, 50 means 50, not an average of 20 and 80.

The more extreme a score, whether it's high or low, the more *modal* it is. In other words, a 20 on a 100-point scale is not likely to be an average of lots of high and low scores but more probably reflects a concentration of low scores. A score that shows such a modal pattern of responses reflects what we call a more *consistent* trait, while a score that shows an average of extremes is a more *situational* (or *polarized*) trait. Extreme scores, such as 30 and below in the lower range and 70 and up in the higher range, typically reflect more consistent behaviors on a trait, while midrange scores, say, between 35 and 65, could reflect either consistent or situational behavior, depending on the individual's makeup. In Figure 7.1, the dotted line represents consistent behaviors at all levels of a trait; the solid line represents the increasing possibility of situational behavior as scores on a trait approach the midrange.

Blends

Blends occur when two or more traits (either factors or facets) interact with each other in such a way that a new trait emerges. This new trait has a life of its own, in that it consists of more than just the characteristics of the component traits taken together. A good example would be the combinative effect of a blend of high N (especially N2, intensity) and low A (especially A2, agreement), which results in the trait of antagonism.

Blends occur both within and between factors. For example, within the E factor, E1 (enthusiasm) and E2 (sociability) combine to create the trait of friendliness. A person who is high in both A and E would be described as nurturing, one who is high in E and O as overbearing. As we will see in Chapter Ten, the ideal form of leadership is a blend of N–, E+, O+, A–, and C+. The results of these blends can produce a variety of effects in values, behaviors, attitudes, roles, needs, motivations, and beliefs.

Multimeaning Terms

Although Gertrude Stein maintained that "a rose is a rose is a rose," few words and behaviors have only one meaning, cause, or effect. Even a rose, given as a gift, could express fondness, love, guilt, a reminiscence, self-indulgence, appreciation of beauty, or simple bribery (when it's a gift with an ulterior motive). In the arena of personality traits, we speak of "multimeaning terms." Take the word *decisiveness*. It sounds like a single personality trait, but it actually has many different possible meanings, each of which represents a separate personality trait. Here are some of these different meanings of *decisiveness* and their associated Big Five traits (each of which is a different pure or blend):

- Knee-jerk decision maker (C–, very spontaneous and lacking in caution)

- Yea-sayer (A+, wanting to please)

- Nay-sayer (A–, competitive and always with a need to be seen as right)

- Driven decision maker (C+, ambitious and focused)

All of these people are decisive, in that they tend to make decisions without delay, but they represent the four distinct traits, or behavioral sets, of spontaneity, acquiescence, antagonism, and ambition.

Nontrait Influences on Traits

In the passage by Gordon Allport at the beginning of this chapter, we heard his insistence that behaviors represent a coming together in time of multiple forces. So although traits clearly exert an influence on behavior, other forces contribute as well. Here is a list of some potential issues that could intensify, modify, or weaken a particular trait, either pure or blended:

Intelligence: Howard Gardner writes of "multiple intelligences," or nine different talents. Possession of auditory or musical talent certainly intensifies exploratory (O+) behavior in the musical realm; lack of kinesthetic talent tends to weaken exploratory behavior in dance and sport. We two authors are both O+ and talented in music, yet lacking in kinesthetic talent. Our exploratory behavior is strained in the presence of dance or sport, yet fully expressed in most areas of music and sound. (See more on aspects of intelligence in Howard [2000c], chap. 22.)

Socioeconomic status: Feeling the obligation to earn more money to support a family can force an individual to take a job that requires unnatural behavior. For example, many people accept promotions into management without the requisite personality infrastructure. The bleak necessity of earning more money can force a person who is E–C– to attempt to maintain an E+C+ profile. Unfortunately, continuing to behave in such an unnatural manner for long periods can be harmful to one's health.

Religious values: A deeply held religious belief in the primacy of one's sect can turn an otherwise friendly person into a judging, intolerant one.

Special and/or temporary circumstances: The character Dunstan Ramsay, a teacher in a fictional private school in Robertson Davies's *Fifth Business,* lamented that "the war [WWII] made good men so scarce that they appointed me [as headmaster], as we must all shoulder our burdens without thought of self. It was taxing, thankless work, and I hated all the administrative side of it. But I bent to the task and did what I could until 1947" (1970, p. 222). This is the lament of an O+ having to behave as an O–.

Job design: The way a job is designed can work with or against certain traits. For example, research has shown that, in general, C+ workers tend to get higher performance appraisals. However, when C– workers are in jobs that have relatively little autonomy, they perform much better than they would in jobs with more autonomy. When they're given wide discretion in how to do a job, they're less successful in the traditional sense. They tend to get sidetracked, to procrastinate. When they're constrained to follow a straight and narrow path, they don't fall victim to their natural tendencies as easily.

Balance between family, social life, and job: We recently talked with a woman who was the director of training with a large organization.

She was also the mother of three school-age children and active in her church. Her Big Five profile included E+O+. She questioned the E+, saying that when she finished work and put the kids to bed she was exhausted and just craved isolation with a good book. Looking at her scores and considering the amount of practical work, lacking intellectual stimulation, that she had to conduct every day, we suggested that at the end of the day she wasn't really tired, but merely bored. What she craved was not isolation and quiet, but an adventure of the mind. This was a significant insight for her, and she committed herself to finding more ways to make work, church, and child rearing more supportive of her need for imagination, novelty, and complexity.

An understanding of the nature of greatness: Some five centuries apart, Niccolò Machiavelli and Mihalyi Csikszentmihalyi wrote about what it takes to be truly great. Machiavelli, in *The Prince*, argued that the best leader needs to do what it takes to get the job done. If a leader needs to be tough, he or she should be tough, but if a situation calls for tenderness, then the leader should be tender. Machiavelli argued that unsuccessful leaders are those who are so rigid that they can't perform the critical aspects of the role. In a similar vein, Csikszentmihalyi (1996) studied several hundred creative geniuses who made major changes in the way their respective fields were conceived: painters, mathematicians, athletes, business leaders, and scientists. He found that they shared one tendency: they did what it took to get the job done, even if it required a behavior that was less than appealing. If careful, tedious proofreading was required, they would do it. They didn't just do the fun, or natural, stuff.

We praise water and fish separately for their unique contributions to the quality of our life. But we also like what they can do synergistically when they join forces. In a sense, the preceding five chapters were about fish and water (that is, separate traits), while the remainder of the book is about combining them, as in beautiful aquariums, bouillabaisse, chowder, water-cleaning algae-eating environmentalists, mousse, and all the other possibilities.

Part
Two

Real-World
Applications
for
Individual
and
Organizational
Performance

The Big Five at Work

Leadership

More Steak, Less Sizzle

For over two millennia, Ulysses, aka Odysseus, has come to our lips when we are asked to name an example of leadership. In the closing three lines of his poem in tribute to this traveler-king, Tennyson pegs the qualities that attest to Ulysses' leadership reputation. Remarkably, or rather, delightfully, Tennyson has penned phrases that parallel the recent findings of Big Five research about the qualities of successful leaders: "equal temper" (N–), "heroic hearts" (E+), "to seek" (O+), "to strive . . . and not to yield" (A–), "strong in will" and "to find" (C+).

Here is the perfect portrait of the leader, corroborated by dozens of studies throughout the last two decades. Although it's possible to succeed as a leader with a different profile, the natural leader defined in Big Five terms is resilient (N–); energetic, outgoing, and persuasive (E+); visionary (O+); competitive (A–); and dedicated to a goal (C+).

What Is Leadership?

If we know what personality traits are associated with the ideal leader, surely we also know what leadership is! Although hundreds of definitions pepper the business literature, including one of our own, probably the most common theme among these definitions is reflected by Hogan, Curphy, and Hogan in their article entitled "What We Know About Leadership" (1994, p. 493): "Leadership involves persuading other people to set aside for a period of time their individual concerns and to pursue a common goal that is important for the responsibilities and welfare of a group."

It was Machiavelli who pointed out that the leader could not be successful by leaning on a single set of extreme behaviors. In *The Prince,* he suggested that one can gain a leadership position through birth, skill, fortune, or force, but that in order to keep the position the leader must be willing to be both a Fox and a Lion. By "Fox," he meant shrewd, and by "Lion," strong (the typical leader). The Fox can be generous yet thrifty, merciful yet just, trusting yet skeptical, restrained yet bold, serious yet frivolous, cautious yet impetuous. The leader who only exhibits the first trait in each pair will be viewed as weak and will be disrespected. The leader who exhibits only the second trait will be hated; he or she will have the power without the glory. As Machiavelli said at one point, the best fortress of a leader is not to be hated, and the Lion, who focuses only on the so-called "strong" behaviors—always being bold, for example, and seeing restraint as a sign of weakness—risks being hated. Machiavelli suggested that the shrewd Fox is able to draw from either pair of behaviors based on what the situation calls for. By presenting a balance, by being willing to draw on complementary resources and not just those that feel natural, this leader can be loved, yet will be appropriately feared; she or he will have the power *and* the glory. The Lion must play the Fox from time to time.

Taking this to heart, leaders, who are generally calm (N–), must be capable of occasionally showing agitation (N+) so that people don't regard them as unfeeling. Though they are generally outgoing and assertive (E+), they must occasionally retire in solitude (E–), or others may conclude that they're uncomfortable with themselves. They may espouse a vision (O+), but they must also be practical and efficient (O–) so that people don't think they're out of touch with reality. Though they can be unyielding (A–), they must be nurturing on occasion (A+) to avoid being accused of greed and arrogance. And though they are generally focused on the goal (C+), they must occasionally be spontaneous and playful (C–), or others may conclude that they're headed for a breakdown.

This pattern is presented as a Big Five profile in Figure 8.1. Subsequent leader profiles will be compared to this standard.

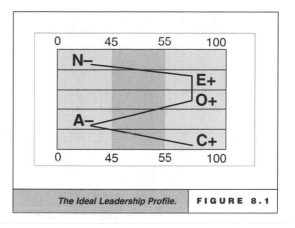

The Ideal Leadership Profile.   **FIGURE 8.1**

The Furnham Study

As an example of how the research literature supports this Big Five leadership profile, consider the Furnham leadership study, which was composed of 160 mid- to upper-level managers in a multinational communications organization. These leaders were anywhere from their late thirties to their mid-fifties in age. Ten licensed psychologists, who were also management consultants, were trained to use an assessment center format to evaluate these 160 managers on ten key leadership abilities. In the assessment center format, assessors (here, the ten licensed psychologists) used a variety of methods (questionnaires, case studies, role plays, and so forth) to assess small groups of individuals on a discrete number of criteria. The NEO PI-R was administered to the managers. Furnham and his team then tried to determine whether the scores on the Big Five were systematically associated with the scores on the ten leadership abilities. As Table 8.1 clearly illustrates, all ten abilities showed strong associations with the Big Five factors and facets.

The results suggest that these ten leadership abilities each require a certain personality infrastructure for their fullest realization. Although the traits identified in Table 8.1 are not mandatory for high performance in the associated leadership ability areas, they certainly make it more likely that an individual will be able to excel in those areas. They are neither necessary nor sufficient, but certainly facilitative. One interesting finding of the Furnham study was that, in

TABLE 8.1 The NEO PI-R Infrastructure for Leadership.

Trait	Drive to Achieve	Drive to Lead	Conceptual Ability	Intuition	Interpersonal Sensitivity	Social Adaptability	Optimism	Resilience	Interest in Business	Internal Locus of Control
N: Negative Emotionality	–	–					– –	– – – – –		– – –
N1: Worry							–	– – – – –		– – –
N2: Anger	–	–			+		–	– –		
N3: Discouragement						–	– –	– – – – –		–
N4: Self-consciousness		–						– – –		–
N5: Impulsiveness	–							– – –		–
N6: Vulnerability	++	– – –					–	– – –		+
E: Extraversion		+		+	+	++	++		+	
E1: Warmth				–	+	++	+		+	
E2: Gregariousness		++		+		+		+	+	++++
E3: Assertiveness	+	++	+	+		+	++		+	++
E4: Activity	+	+	+	++			++		+	
E5: Excitement seeking			+	++						
E6: Positive emotions				+	+	+	++		+	
O: Openness				++		++				
O1: Fantasy				+		+		–		
O2: Aesthetics				++				+		
O3: Feelings				++	++		+	+		
O4: Actions				+				–		
O5: Ideas	+		+	++		+			+	
O6: Values				+			+			
A: Agreeableness					++					
A1: Trust	–	–			+					
A2: Straightforwardness		–								
A3: Altruism		– –			+	+	+			–
A4: Compliance	–	– –			+					
A5: Modesty	–			+	+					
A6: Tender-mindedness					+					
C: Conscientiousness	+++	+						++		
C1: Competence	++	++					++	+	++	++
C2: Order	++						+	+	++	++
C3: Dutifulness	+									+
C4: Achievement striving	++	++						+		+
C5: Self-discipline	++	+					++	+	+	++
C6: Deliberation	++						++	+		++

Source: Adrian Furnham, John Crump, and Josh Whelan, "Validating the NEO Personality Inventory Using Assessors' Ratings," *Personality and Individual Differences,* 22(5), 1997, pp. 669–675.

their culture, the A factor lacked consistency in its relation to the ten competencies. Most strikingly, A– was associated with "Drive to Lead" and "Drive to Achieve," while A+ was associated with "Interpersonal Sensitivity." This is known as a trade-off, in which it is next to impossible to find both qualities in the same person, except in some watered-down or moderate degree. If you want a leader with strong drive, you must typically sacrifice some interpersonal sensitivity; if you want a leader with strong interpersonal sensitivity, you must sacrifice some amount of drive. A leader who is moderate in A will tend to have moderate interpersonal skills (unless E is high) and moderate drive (unless C is very high). Therefore, carefully identifying the needs of a specific role prior to selecting or appointing a leader will help in determining what trade-offs, if any, are necessary.

Must Leaders Have a Perfect Score?

If we know the ideal, optimal, or target infrastructure profile for leadership, then what are the consequences when a leader has a profile that is off-target? If a leader matches the ideal on all but one or two dimensions, what are the specific liabilities and how does the leader compensate for them? In Table 8.2, we summarize the key benefits, concerns, and remedies based on whether or not an individual leader scores on-target, to the right of the target (above, or in excess of, the optimum), or to the left of the target (below the optimum) on the Big Five as it relates to leadership. The optimum score on a 100-point standard score scale is identified after the dimension label in the first column.

Note that an excess or deficiency in a particular dimension can be offset, or moderated, by compensating scores in related dimensions. For example, O+ can be tamed by C+, A– can be smoothed over by E+ and N–, N– can be made expressive by E+ and either A+ or A–, and the coolness of E– can be warmed up by the nurturing qualities of A+. By looking for such interactive effects, we can avoid the trap of assuming that an extreme score on one dimension has automatic and inevitable effects. An O+ person will always be imaginative, but the trait will appear differently when the same person is E+ (overbearing), A– (entrepreneurial), or C– (impractical).

TABLE 8.2 *The Optimum Big Five Leadership Profile, with Benefits, Concerns, and Remedies for Those Who Do and Do Not Match the Profile.*

Dimension	To the Left of Optimum	Optimum (Plus or Minus 5 Points)	To the Right of Optimum
N (45)	*Benefits:* Many; Resilient; perceived as eternally calm and unflappable; extremely difficult to unnerve; inspires high confidence.	*Benefits:* Borderline Resilient and Responsive; calm, cool, and collected when needed; recovers quickly from crises; inspires confidence among subordinates that the leader is durable and will prevail; shows appropriate concern from time to time.	*Benefits:* Few; Reactive: on occasion, reactivity will show subordinates that the leader is human.
	Concerns: On occasion, can communicate coolness or indifference.	*Concerns:* None.	*Concerns:* Many; wariness, a tendency to worry, self-consciousness, and/or temper tend to eat away at the confidence of subordinates.
	Remedies: Make it a point to communicate, in speech or in writing, all positive and negative feedback to your followers.	*Remedies:* No need.	*Remedies:* Learn the arts of meditation, isometrics, deep breathing; take aerobic exercise; deal aggressively with sources of stress.
E (55)	*Benefits:* Few; Introvert; excels in a paperwork-intensive leadership position; is more accepted in highly introverted cultures, such as accounting, information technology, engineering.	*Benefits:* Borderline Ambivert and Extravert; friendly, approachable, gregarious, assertive, enthusiastic; natural communicator face-to-face; is comfortable taking charge.	*Benefits:* Many; Extravert; practices management by wandering around; enjoys being in the thick of things; handles a heavy meeting schedule well; enjoys meeting and greeting and networking; is good in a highly extraverted culture, such as sales.
	Concerns: Many; has a tendency to under-communicate; minimizes meetings; avoids the spotlight.	*Concerns:* None.	*Concerns:* Few; resists closing the door and churning out the necessary paperwork; can tire out teammates if they are more introverted.
	Remedies: Delegate meeting facilitation to another, more extraverted team member; increase use of written communication, especially for informal matters (recognition, constructive criticism, reminders).	*Remedies:* No need.	*Remedies:* Establish a "quiet hour" in which you are protected from interruptions; resist interrupting others.

O (55)

Benefits: Few; Preserver; concerned with tactics; focuses on the details (especially when E− and C+); typically good as a project manager; typically better as a manager in a maintenance or status quo situation where little change is required.

Concerns: Tends to focus on the here and now, rather than on the big picture and future needs; minimizes the need for change.

Remedies: Invite an associate, vendor, or customer who is O+ to come in from time to time and challenge your assumptions about the short and long term.

Benefits: Borderline Moderate and Explorer; appropriately imaginative; anticipates future needs; focuses on strategy; handles theory, complexity, and uncertainty well; embraces change when the situation calls for it.

Concerns: None.

Remedies: No need.

Benefits: Many; Explorer; naturally creative and imaginative; comfortable focusing on theory, complex problems, and the future; sees opportunities for change as enjoyable.

Concerns: May enjoy change for change's sake; may resist spending sufficient time on the details; if C−, will have difficulty being on time and within budget; will probably get bored if management responsibilities don't challenge the imagination.

Remedies: Have an assistant or close associate who has permission to ride herd on you with respect to being practical and meeting stated objectives.

A (45)

Benefits: Depends on the values of the organizational culture; Challenger; in tougher, more competitive situations, will rarely back down from a challenge; tough-minded; independent; thick-skinned (if also N−); enjoys center stage (especially if also N− and E+); enjoys a good fight.

Concerns: Can come across as arrogant, untrusting, and superior; can alienate team members; plays to win; has frequent conflicts.

Remedies: Be willing to reconsider any decision made in the heat of the moment; take aerobic exercise before meetings in which you need to soften your approach; have an associate who has permission to give you feedback when your ego has exceeded accepted norms.

Benefits: Borderline Challenger and Negotiator; good negotiator; goes for the win-win approach; is sufficiently tough, but able also to show understanding of others' needs and interests; can wheel and deal without either caving in to others or crushing them.

Concerns: None.

Remedies: No need.

Benefits: Depends on the values of the organizational culture; Adapter; can excel in a friendly, trusting, nurturing environment that emphasizes teamwork and cooperation.

Concerns: is subject to being duped, tricked, and outmaneuvered by associates, vendors, or customers who are more competitive and manipulative; doesn't like to fight and avoids conflict.

Remedies: Identify an associate or consultant who can assist you in negotiations or other situations in which you know you must stand up to people who play hardball.

TABLE 8.2	Continued.		
Dimension	To the Left of Optimum	Optimum (Plus or Minus 5 Points)	To the Right of Optimum
	Benefits: Very few; Flexible; is spontaneous and enjoys wearing different hats; can serve well in a staff-type management position that must respond to a variety of ever-changing needs from line management.	*Benefits:* Borderline Balanced and Focused; tends to stay organized with minimal effort; disciplined; ambitious; naturally stays focused on immediate and long-term priorities and goals; is appropriately cautious in decision making; has high standards for self and others; is likely to have balanced professional and personal lives.	*Benefits:* Many; Focused; very ambitious; highly disciplined and difficult, if not impossible, to distract from the task or goal at hand; strong preference for finishing one project before beginning another; a perfectionist who maintains very high standards; someone who can always be trusted to deliver what is promised.
C (55)	*Concerns:* Lacks discipline, organization, and ambition; can work hard and long, but is easily distracted from immediate or long-term goals.	*Concerns:* None.	*Concerns:* Often is a workaholic who causes associates lower in C to resent having to match the leader's long hours, untiring drive, and will to achieve; has difficulty flexing when the goal changes or is put on hold.
	Remedies: You can excel when the job is highly structured with minimal allowance for discretion and autonomy; otherwise, you need an associate to ride herd on you to meet deadlines, attend to details, avoid distractions, and stick to the budget.	*Remedies:* No need.	*Remedies:* Understand that your associates do not typically have your high comfort level for long hours and dedication to goals; occasionally take yourself with a grain of salt to show associates that you are aware of your excesses; make a point of being playful or spontaneous to appear more human to your associates and family when it won't jeopardize your goal attainment.

Leadership Case Study 1
The Training Officers

We had the privilege recently of profiling a team of twenty-five U.S. military officers at the rank of captain or above, including one general class officer. These military service professionals were all involved in the delivery of training topics from nursing to lock picking. They weren't required to design the training; instead, they prepared instructors to deliver the training, monitored its quality, and maintained a state of readiness to deliver the training during peacetime, national emergencies, and war. Given this mission, would you predict that their composite leadership profile was similar to or different from the ideal profile? Because they were staff officers whose mission didn't involve combat duty or normal line duties, we would expect their A scores to be slightly higher than normal, with an emphasis on interpersonal sensitivity. In addition, since they didn't have to design the training (which would be associated with O+) and were more involved with tactical management issues than strategic ones, we expected their O scores to be a tad lower than the ideal. And that's exactly what we found, as you can see from their composite profile in Figure 8.2.

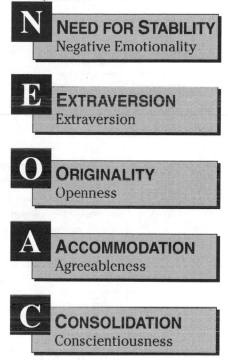

N NEED FOR STABILITY
Negative Emotionality

E EXTRAVERSION
Extraversion

O ORIGINALITY
Openness

A ACCOMMODATION
Agreeableness

C CONSOLIDATION
Conscientiousness

Leadership Case Study 2
The NBA Coach Who Fell Short

Another profile we had the privilege of obtaining was that of a National Basketball Association head coach. This

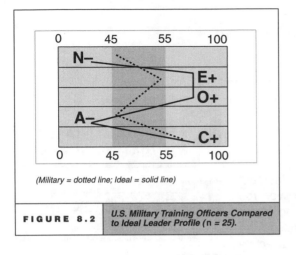

0   45   55   100

N–

E+

O+

A–

C+

0   45   55   100

(Military = dotted line; Ideal = solid line)

FIGURE 8.2 | *U.S. Military Training Officers Compared to Ideal Leader Profile (n = 25).*

gentleman was well-liked and had basketball savvy, yet he lacked what it took to get close to the championship. His Big Five profile provided some insight as to the reason. As you can see from his profile in Figure 8.3, he was O+ and C+, which matched his basketball savvy (he was an excellent strategist and was known for creative playmaking) and his ambition (he was disciplined and focused). However, note his elevated N, lower E, and higher A in comparison to the ideal leader. The result: he was a worrier, and apparently this translated to his players as low confidence in himself and them. In addition, he was an Ambivert, so he was more private than was desirable in this leadership position and spent less time with his players face-to-face; thus he didn't offer his players the parental type of guidance and presence that is so necessary to young millionaires who haven't yet grown up. Finally, he was moderate in A, which supported his excellent interpersonal sensitivity but not the essential toughness needed to take on the strong egos of rich, know-it-all NBA pros.

Leadership Case Study 3
The Uncommunicative VP

For the third and final profile, we present the vice president for administration of a manufacturing company in the Midwest. Responsible for some twelve people involved in bookkeeping, computer technology, local-area-network support, accounts payable and receivable, and budgeting, he was getting deeper and deeper into trouble. When we were called in to intervene, several of his subordinates had quit, others were threatening to quit, and the department's morale was at an all-time low. Accusations of favoritism and bias against women and minorities were rampant. We interviewed each department member as a way of gaining an understanding of the situation. When we asked what the typical department meetings were like, we were met with "What department meetings? We haven't had a department meeting in over three years!" And when we asked the department members how the vice president communicated with them, they said, "What communication? We get maybe one e-mail a week. Occasionally, when he thinks people have screwed up, he walks back here, rakes them over the coals, and gives them an ultimatum to fix the problem. Otherwise, we never see or hear from him."

Now let's take a look at this leader-yet-not-a-leader. His profile is provided in Figure 8.4. You can quickly see the problem. Although he had the requisite N– and C+ and a satisfactory O=, he was off the chart on E– and A–. The result was a strongly introverted person who believed he was always right

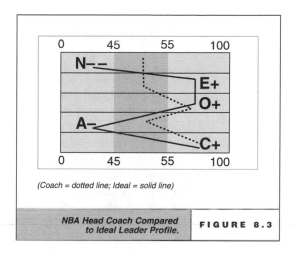

(Coach = dotted line; Ideal = solid line)

NBA Head Coach Compared to Ideal Leader Profile.   **FIGURE 8.3**

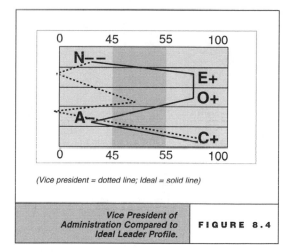

(Vice president = dotted line; Ideal = solid line)

Vice President of Administration Compared to Ideal Leader Profile.   **FIGURE 8.4**

and who had zero relationship skills. When he was interviewed, he said that he prided himself on not having taken one day of vacation in five years, and he arrogantly thought less of associates who had. He was subsequently counseled to get out of management. He became a corporate troubleshooter, as he was quite competent in what he did, and they all lived happily ever after.

A Final Word About Leadership and Personality

No magic set of scores equates to good leadership; nor must a leader be ineffective just because one or two scores fall short of the ideal. The fact that some people have an ideal profile for leadership doesn't mean that those who don't should be excluded from the opportunity to lead. Instead, the ideal profile highlights important characteristics of leadership that need to be addressed in some way. Introverted leaders can excel in any situation, but it will be more natural (and comfortable) for them to work in a more introverted environment. In addition, as we'll see in Chapter Sixteen, leaders can employ a wide variety of strategies to offset the effects of traits that fall short of the ideal. Where a will exists, a way is possible.

Selling and Influencing

How to Build Rapport

With seven brief words, Willy Loman's oldest son highlights the essence of the problem of how to influence others: influence them to buy from you, to agree with you, to give you favorable attention or consideration, to establish rapport with you—in short, to give you the time of day. Research on influence currently suggests that the prerequisite for influencing others is self-knowledge (knowing your "rock bottom," your strengths and weaknesses), not keeping up appearances ("a smile and a shoeshine"). In this chapter we will explore the importance of knowing both your rock bottom and the rock bottom of the people you would like to influence.

The word *influence* conveys the sense of one entity flowing out into or onto another. *Influence* refers, for example, to the river's impact, or influence, on the land its waters are flowing onto, or irrigating. To have influence, then, is to have your essence strike a resonating response in the essence of another person, to render that person different as a result of having come in contact with you, to cause him or her to grow or change in some way, just as river water makes land more fertile. Henry Melville, an eighteenth-century English diplomat, once described it this way: "A thousand fibers connect us with our fellow-man; and along those fibers, as sympathetic threads, our actions run as causes, and they come back to us as effects."

Influence is the process of matching my behavior to yours: when in Green Bay, cheer for the Packers. Similarly, if I wish to influence a gregarious person, I should find a genuine way to be gregarious with that person. Most of us like to look in the mirror and see ourselves. Most of us like to look at another person and see someone like us. Finding these common fibers, or traits, is affirming and gratifying and tends to establish rapport and promote acceptance. If I'm gregarious and enjoy "doing lunch" and am asked by someone to do lunch, assuming that I don't deeply detest that person, I'll be pleased to accept. I think, "You're like me [that is, we both like to do lunch]! Let's get to know each other better." But first things first. Before we can plot strategies based on the ways in which we're similar to or different from other people, we need to learn how to recognize others' traits—the ways in which they are like us or different from us.

How to Quickly Figure Out a Subject's Traits

We are seldom able to give a personality inventory to someone whose profile we want to determine. In lieu of having another person's personality test scores, the next best thing is to estimate what part of each Big Five continuum this person, whom we shall call the "subject," best reflects: more extraverted, more introverted, or somewhere in between. As an aid in making this estimate, we provide the observable clues listed in Table 9.1. This table includes four different kinds of clues: behavior, language, values, and environment (office, car, dress, and person). Note that some clues appear for more than one dimension. If a person possesses all the traits associated with a clue, the clue is that much more accurate; for example, security is an important value for individuals who are A+ and those who are C+, but it is doubly important to individuals who are both A+ and C+. Asterisks in the table indicate clues that research shows to be especially strongly associated with a particular trait; for example, benevolence is highly valued by people who are high in A. However, an individual would be unlikely to exhibit *all* the clues in any given row. Relatively few individuals in the world are examples of a pure, prototypical trait. Remember, traits do not really exist; they're merely sets of correlated behaviors. Relatively correlated, not absolutely correlated.

We should be aware that personality traits are comprised of opposite behaviors that serve to offset each other but that are not mutually exclusive in a person. To be gregarious means to be gregarious *most* of the time, not *all* the time. To be solitary means to be solitary *most* of the time, not *all* the time. We each have our natural preferences, but we are capable of exhibiting the opposing, balancing behaviors. Losing the capability of drawing upon both extremes signals the onset of a psychological disorder. Recall Haemon's advice to his father, Creon, king of Thebes, in Sophocles' *Antigone:* "Seest thou, beside the wintry torrent's course, how the trees that yield to it save every twig, while the stiff-necked perish root and branch?" (Jebb translation, lines 708–710). All work and no play makes Jack an obsessive-compulsive. All work and *some* play, that's healthy.

The fact that all of us can draw upon each extreme of each trait is what makes the concept of influence strategies legitimate. Although you may not be a "doing lunch" type of person, you do have it in you to do lunch with a more extraverted person with relish and sincerity, though you wouldn't like to do it as frequently as would the Extravert you're trying to influence.

The Trait-Based Influence Process

Now that we know how to determine a subject's likely personality profile, we can take a look at the seven steps of the influence process. The same process applies to selling, negotiating, and persuading. The goal of the process is to use behaviors that establish maximum rapport with your subject.

1. *Identify the subject's salient traits:* Each of us has one or more salient traits. In order to determine those of your subject, you must have one of three things: the subject's Big Five test scores, very good natural instincts for spotting personality traits, or Table 9.1. Whichever method you employ, the "scores" on one or more of the traits will probably be higher

TABLE 9.1   Clues for Estimating a Subject's Position on the Big Five Continua.

Dimension/ Continuum	Behavior	Language	Values	Environment (Office, Car, Dress, Person)
More Reactive (N+)	Is a smoker Is quick to anger Is excitable Is anxious Is extreme in eye contact (gazers and averters) Is somewhat uncomfortable in front of others Is more easily embarrassed, shy Shows signs of discouragement	Tempo changes Makes comments about bodily discomforts Has a tendency to interrupt Finds it harder to say no and resist urges	Tranquility Universalism, social justice, welfare of all	Sits or stands at a greater distance Easily slips into road rage Is more likely to be and/or appear to be physically out of condition
More Resilient (N−)	Remains calm throughout meetings Recovers quickly from crises Has a normal amount of eye contact Is slow to anger Is comfortable in front of others Is less easily embarrassed Doesn't show signs of discouragement	Speaks with a controlled pace and vocabulary Finds it easier to say no and resist urges	Rationality; keeping emotions subdued	Sits or stands at a closer distance Is unfazed by other drivers' idiocies Wears more subdued clothing Is more likely to be physically fit
More Extraverted (E+)	Is good at greeting people Is warm and friendly Is less inhibited Makes more eye contact Is an initiator and responder Takes longer strides Uses more caffeine in the morning Is optimistic and cheerful Has a vigorous pace; likes excitement	Talks louder, faster, longer Is impatient with slower speech Is likely to talk "on top of" someone else Responds better to more aggressive humor	Achievement, ambition, success, competence* Power, wealth, authority, social status Self-direction, creativity, independent thought Stimulation, variety in life, novelty, excitement Universalism, social justice, welfare of all	Is more active; doesn't remain at desk or station Keeps the door open Office is "busier," more colorful Sits facing the door Tends to sit opposite people Dresses for the occasion

More Introverted (E–)	Is comfortable reading while you wait Is more sedentary Has less eye contact Is more inhibited Is an observer Tends to sit at right angles Takes shorter strides Uses less caffeine in the morning	Pauses and thinks before speaking Is hard to read; is less assertive Talks less and more briefly than most Is unlikely to "talk 'on top of' someone else Enjoys more subtle humor	Tradition, humility, respect, commitment Privacy	Is more sedentary Keeps the door closed Sits with back to the door Office environment is quiet, subdued Is leisurely, reserved; stays in the background Is an independent dresser
More Exploring (O+)	Is curious about a wide range of topics Is easily bored Is more likely to have pursued multiple careers throughout life Is less bound by rules and more playful Responds to more unusual humor	Speech is more colorful and entertaining Uses more gestures when talking Language and thinking are more future-oriented Talks and thinks in terms of concepts Emphasizes the uniqueness of products and services	Hedonism, pleasure, enjoyment, sensuousness Achievement, ambition, success, competence Power, wealth, authority, social status Self-direction, creativity, independent thought* Stimulation, variety in life, novelty, excitement	Has more unusual furniture and decor Appears busy; has many stacks and books Frequently changes and redecorates the work space Prefers a variety of projects Tends to prefer modern and abstract art Wears more colorful and festive clothing
More Preserving (O–)	Is punctual Tends to go by the rules Has a narrow range of interests Is committed to only one career Is more serious Shows little or no interest in the arts Prefers the familiar the tried and true	Responds to more mainstream humor Expresses more conservative views; prefers the status quo and resists change Talks about today, not tomorrow; is not a futurist	Tradition, humility, respect, commitment* Conformity, obedience, restraint in actions	Prefers standard furniture and equipment Uses patriotic paraphernalia Uses neutral colors; decor is often ordinary Wall hangings depict action, plants, products Wears conservative clothing

Note: * = clues that are strongly associated with a particular trait.

TABLE 9.1 Continued.

Dimension/ Continuum	Behavior	Language	Values	Environment (Office, Car, Dress, Person)
More Adaptive (A+)	Enjoys being helpful Is concerned about others' opinions and reactions Is warm and friendly	Tends to agree, or at least not disagree, with most assertions Appears to take you at your word, without checking for proof or detail Wants to know who else is using or doing the same thing Talks about how people will react	Security, reciprocity, safety, harmony Universalism, social justice, welfare of all Benevolence, loyalty, welfare of those who are close* Conformity, obedience, restraint in actions Tradition, humility, respect, commitment	Has family memorabilia in evidence Observes traffic rules and laws such as speed limits and no-parking zones Clothing tends to follow the local code
More Challenging (A−)	Is tough-minded; shows little sympathy Prefers conventional gender roles Is brash; is sensitive only to get something	Is an aggressive question asker Is skeptical; doesn't take things at face value Uses expressive language, including expletives and vulgarities Is argumentative	Hedonism, pleasure, enjoyment, sensuousness Power, wealth, authority, social status Self-direction, creativity, independent thought	Is willing to decorate in a daring way; doesn't seek approval Displays evidence of pride in accomplishments, such as trophies, degrees, awards, and certificates Slips into road rage Disregards traffic rules such as speed limits and no-parking zones Clothing makes a statement and is daring

More Focused **(C+)**	Is punctual Tends to go by the rules Always acts professionally Consistently uses personal organizer Is reliable; follows through or promises Allots time for meetings with people and adjourns when the time has run out Sees life as consisting of tasks to accomplish; is goal-oriented Prefers to finish one task or project before starting another; is a serial processor Focuses on the details	Pushes for clarity and closure: "What's next?" Clarifies the agenda up front: "Here's what we're going to discuss and accomplish in this meeting."* Talks about alternatives and consequences	Tradition, humility, respect, commitment Achievement, ambition, success, competence Security, reciprocity, safety, harmony Universalism, social justice, welfare of all Conformity, obedience, restraint in actions	Is neat; has everything in its place (sometimes in stacks) Lets others screen calls; lets voice mail pick up calls Car is typically free of any clutter Always looks professional Has better health habits
More Flexible **(C−)**	Takes work home Sees life as a series of processes; is role-oriented Sees life as consisting of pleasures to be experienced Is comfortable switching from one task or activity to another; is a parallel processor Is content to "wing it" without an agenda Is prone to neglect follow-through Is spontaneous, even knee-jerk, in responding to people	Is easily interrupted and isn't bothered by it Is happy to reopen old issues	Hedonism, pleasure, enjoyment, sensuousness Stimulation, variety in life, novelty, excitement	Shows evidence of disorganization; may hide clutter in desk or car trunk before important meetings Is easily distracted by competing events Will take calls and allow interruptions while meeting with people Car is likely to be strewn with papers, pencils, food, cups Is casual about clothing and appearance Has poorer health habits

Note: * = clues that are strongly associated with a particular trait.

than the others. The clearest, strongest trait is the salient trait. If you're using Table 9.1 to determine a person's salient trait or traits, you need to review the clues for both the high (+) and low (–) versions of each of the Big Five traits. If neither row is clearly more descriptive of the subject, then neither is a salient trait. A salient trait only emerges when one row of clues clearly resembles the subject more than its paired row.

2. *Determine compatible and incompatible salient traits:* For this step, you need to know your rock bottom, your salient traits. Compare your salient traits with those of your subject. If your subject is an Introvert and you are an Extravert, the two traits are incompatible. If your subject and you are both Flexibles, the traits are compatible. If you are an Explorer and your subject is a Moderate (midrange), the traits are compatible, with the warning that you may tend to overdo O+ behavior.

3. *Review strategies for your compatible traits:* Table 9.2 lists some of the natural influence strategies for each extreme of the five personality factors. These strategies are based on the natural behaviors for each of the ten complementary traits. For example, since doing lunch is a natural E+ behavior, it becomes a natural strategy to use as part of an overall plan to have influence with an E+ subject. As part of her research for her doctoral dissertation, Lucinda Blue (1999) worked with us to confirm that these natural influence strategies were the strategies of choice for people who scored in each of the extreme ranges of the Big Five. For this step of the process, review the natural strategies listed in Table 9.2 for salient traits that you and your subject share. Shared traits include instances in which you and your subject have the same extreme trait (for example, both of you are A–), as well as instances in which one of you has an extreme trait and the other is midrange on the same dimension (for example, the subject is A– and you are A=). Shared salient traits form the most natural basis for establishing rapport between two people, because they involve behaviors that are natural and enjoyable for both parties. Make a list of the natural strategies that make the most sense for the situation at hand.

Some Natural Strategies for the Ten Complementary Traits, Derived from Their Associated Behaviors.	**TABLE 9.2**

Trait	Natural Influence Strategies	
Resilient **(N–)**	Use a setting that's fresh with appropriate background stimulation, such as a park. Avoid excessive distances (for example, take the closer chair). Use logic and reasonableness.	Make your limits clear. Don't interrupt them. Use a problem-solving method or structure. Ask how they see the alternatives and build on mutual ones.
Reactive **(N ↑)**	Minimize distractions (noise, music, activity). Maximize the distance between you (for example, avoid the nearest chair). Appeal to their pride in their organization and family.	Take their stress seriously but not personally. Minimize your reliance on logic and reasonableness. Emphasize what's in it for them. Show the appropriate emotion to support your position.
Introvert **(E–)**	Rely on memos and letters. Try to match their energy level when it's lower than yours. Don't rush them; allow them time to readjust. Allow or even initiate a move toward greater privacy. Resist your urge to draw in other people. Use ample visual cues. Use nonphysical rewards, such as honorary degrees.	Allow them time to read and have moments of silence. Don't get too close physically. Appeal to their uniqueness as a person. Avoid sexual and aggressive humor; use subtlety. Remind them of the names of things. Make sure they don't become overstimulated.
Extravert **(E+)**	Go out for a meal together. Feel free to telephone. Meet with two or more people at a time. Don't assume they want privacy if their door is closed. Enjoy small talk if they initiate it.	Try to match their high energy in a genuine way (for example, standing or walking when they do). Appeal to their sense of responsibility. Use the promise of physical rewards, such as sports or food.

TABLE 9.2	*Continued.*

Trait	Natural Influence Strategies	
Preserver (O−)	Emphasize the tried-and-true aspects of your proposal. Walk them through your proposal step-by-step (use flowcharts). Play up to their need to compete and win. Don't waste their time; be specific; give examples. Emphasize the simple and easy-to-use aspects of your proposal. Refer to established companies that have used your product or idea.	Emphasize your idea's positive impact on efficiency. Use mainstream humor, but be generally serious. Avoid appealing to novelty and curiosity. Avoid a complex vocabulary that isn't common to their specialty. Appeal to established, traditional values. Emphasize conformity with policies and procedures.
Explorer (O+)	Don't oversimplify. Refer to the individuals who developed the idea or product. Emphasize the uniqueness of the idea or product. Use metaphors to describe the idea or product. Take your time. Let them take credit where possible. Appreciate their unusual sense of humor. Refer to the theory behind the application.	Appeal to their need to innovate. Avoid concentrating on details; give the big picture first. Ask questions about their opinions and ideas. Get agreement on specifics, yet be prepared for them to change their minds. Appeal to their curiosity; use reason and logic.
Challenger (A−)	Push for closure on the basis of bottom-line results. Emphasize the logical tightness of your position. Be sure to do what you say you will. Have alternatives drawn out with plans for each. Encourage their criticism and build on their skepticism.	Build on their need to win and to be right. Avoid references to consideration for others. Don't take apparent belligerence personally; be flexible.
Adapter (A+)	Emphasize how specific groups of people will react. Show how your agenda relates to human values. Push for closure on the basis of your proposal's impact on people. Inquire about their family, hobbies, and so forth.	Emphasize the ethical rightness of your proposal. Take the time to develop a relationship. Because of their tendency to defer, ask questions that draw them out. Emphasize how your proposal will help others.

| | Continued. | **TABLE 9.2** |

Trait	Natural Influence Strategies	
Flexible (C–)	Help them to identify what they need in order to make a decision. Emphasize your flexibility. Summarize the discussion frequently. Be patient if they make you wait or make you late. Permit yourself to be spontaneous; don't rush them. Don't insist on your agenda when they want to veer from it.	Help them to manage their time and priorities. Be willing to wander off in new and different directions. Emphasize the pleasurable aspects of your position. Appeal to their role as a consultant and adviser.
Focused (C+)	Set goals and a point-by-point agenda for the meeting. Be sure to arrive on time or somewhat early. Give as much advance warning about changes of plans as possible. Relate to their good health and record of achievement; identify with their favorite way to exercise. To avoid a premature decision against your position, agree on specific steps for follow-up or future meeting dates.	Notify them if you're going to be late. Emphasize a good work ethic. Be sensitive to their need and respect for structure. Use logic with clearly identified priorities and goals. Emphasize that they are in control.

Source: Based on P. J. Howard and J. M. Howard, *Rapport and Influence Strategies: A Planning Workbook for Enhancing Your Rapport and Influence with Significant Others in Your Personal and Professional Life,* 1997, Charlotte, NC: Center for Applied Cognitive Studies; and Lucinda Blue, "The Relationship Between Personality Traits and Influence Strategies: A Comparison of College Business Students and Business Professionals," unpublished doctoral dissertation, The Union Institute Graduate School, Cincinnati, Ohio, 1999.

4. *Review strategies that are unnatural for you, but natural for your subject:* If your subject is E– and you are E+, then the E– behaviors and strategies listed in Table 9.2 might best be described as *unnatural* for you. Although you certainly can engage in them, they might not be your first choice. However, this step is a significant and effective one in influencing others: for example, do as the Japanese do even though you are not Japanese. International business meetings typically require one party to engage in an "unnatural" behavior, such as bowing, that is natural for the other party. This step of the influence process consists of nothing more

than identifying behaviors that are natural for your subject
(E–) but unnatural for you (E+). If you are a salesperson
and your subject is a purchasing manager, it's highly likely
that your subject is E– and you are E+. Table 9.2 suggests
that E– people typically don't like to be dropped in on, so
you should seriously consider always giving the purchasing
manager ample warning before visiting. Review the natural
strategies for your subject's salient traits on which you score
at the opposite end, and make a list of any strategies that
are unnatural for you but that would make good sense in
the situation.

5. *Review strategies that are unnatural for your subject, but natural for you:* This step is the inverse of the previous one. Here,
you want to take a careful look at the strategies that are natural for you (they are based on a salient trait for you) but
unnatural for your subject (the subject has the opposite
salient trait). For example, in step 4, in which you are an E+
salesperson who wishes to approach an E– purchasing manager, E+ behaviors occur naturally for you but not for the
purchasing manager. Because the purchasing manager is
unlikely to enjoy doing lunch on a regular basis, you should
plan to avoid, or at least minimize, this type of strategy. That
is what Cervantes meant in *Don Quixote* when he referred to
people riding their hobbyhorses—that is, doing what comes
naturally without thinking. Review the list of strategies for
traits that are salient for you but opposed to your subject's
salient traits. Make a list of the strategies that are natural for
you but that you should probably avoid in this situation. For
example, resist the temptation to drop by and do lunch.

6. *Formulate a plan:* Take the three lists you've drawn up in
steps 3 through 5 and formulate a plan. The plan should be
simple, focusing on a handful of behaviors that appear to
make the most sense in this situation. This is not so much a
three-step plan as it is a manageable list of do's and don'ts
for working with this subject.

7. *Periodically evaluate your assumptions:* As you get to know
your subject better, and as you begin to sense her or his
reaction to your selected strategies, you should revisit your

assessment of the subject's likely profile (step 1 above). You may have misidentified a salient trait, or missed a trait that you've since learned is salient. Then review your list of strategies. Add, delete, or modify strategies based on any changes in your assessment of the other person's profile and on your experience with the subject to date. In addition, add strategies that you omitted earlier but that now appear to make sense in the current situation.

How Influence Strategies Relate to Selling

Influence is to sales as style is to writing. A writer can be minimally effective by simply creating a story and a set of characters, but style is what grabs the reader's attention. In parallel fashion, a salesperson can go through the phases of a sales model (prospecting, qualifying, pitching, closing, and so forth), but employing the proper influence strategies is what establishes the rapport necessary for the sales process to work. However, sales consists of more than influence strategies and techniques or models. Research has identified ideal personality profiles for selling and negotiating. The complete package, then, includes the right personality, the right influence strategies, and the right model or technique.

Figure 9.1 portrays what research has discovered to be the most effective sales personality across a variety of situations. Notice that, in most ways, the ideal sales profile is an exaggerated form of the ideal leadership profile (see Figure 8.1). Whereas the leader is moderately resilient (N–), the salesperson benefits from an extra dose of resilience (N– –) in order to bounce back quickly from rejection. Whereas the leader is moderately extraverted (E+), the salesperson benefits from an extra burst of sociability (E++)

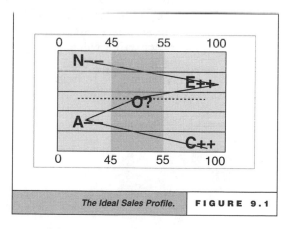

The Ideal Sales Profile.   **FIGURE 9.1**

in order to overcome call reluctance and enjoy the world of "meeting and greeting." An exception to this trend is O, where the ideal salesperson's profile is more industry-specific. In an industry with a complex line of products or services, such as architecture, advertising, or health care services, a salesperson would be more effective with a higher dose of O, in order to be comfortable with the essential uniqueness of every sales call. On the other hand, in an industry with relatively simple products and services, such as widget manufacturing or long distance and cable services, a salesperson would benefit from a low dose of O, in order to be comfortable with the repetitive nature of each sales call.

This pattern, in which the ideal salesperson is a more exaggerated form of the ideal leader, continues with A and C. With lower A, the salesperson can muster the competitiveness, toughness, and pride necessary for daily encounters with resistant prospects and cutthroat competitors. (Note that some corporate and national cultures, such as businesses that provide religious products and services and the cultures of parts of Japan and Asia, tend to be higher in A; A– salespeople would not be effective there.) And the salesperson with higher C will demonstrate the ambition, discipline, and predictability required to take the organization to high levels of growth and profitability.

Certainly a salesperson can succeed in spite of not having the "ideal" profile. However, when the salesperson is in the sales mode, he or she needs to employ the requisite ideal behaviors, even though some may be unnatural. Although you don't have to be naturally resilient (N–) to succeed in sales, it certainly helps. The context also makes a difference. A reactive (N+) salesperson who must face rejection every day but who is greeted at home in the evening by a nurturing partner will certainly fare better than one who is greeted by an antagonistic partner. After hitting "rock bottom," it's nice indeed to have someone to help pick you up.

10

Career Planning

If the Job Fits, Work It

Through his extensive research, The Johns Hopkins University's John Holland has identified six career paths, or styles:

1. *Realistic:* Mechanical and outdoorsy; hands on; not theoretical

2. *Investigative:* Research and inquiry

3. *Artistic:* Writing and the arts

4. *Social:* Working with people; teaching and social work

5. *Enterprising:* Sales and management

6. *Conventional:* Office work and equipment; more sedentary

These six styles form a hexagon, with each point on the hexagon most different in nature from the style opposite it and most similar to the styles adja-

> ❝*God obligeth no man to more than he hath given him ability to perform.*❞
>
> —The Koran

cent to it. Referring to Figure 10.1, we can see that "Realistic" is opposed in nature to "Social," but similar to "Conventional" and "Investigative," which are adjacent to it. Several different lines of research have identified the connection between Holland's hexagon and the Five-Factor Model; these relationships are indicated on Figure 10.1.

Holland's hexagonal model is coordinated with the *Dictionary of Occupational Titles (DOT)* (U.S. Department of Labor, Employment, and Training Administration, 1991), which includes more than twenty thousand brief job descriptions. Once you've figured out the style or styles that are your "rock bottom," you can find literally thousands of job titles with accompanying job descriptions that are populated by people who, for the most part, share your same career style. This relationship between the Big Five, Holland, and the *DOT* is a powerful tool for career planning and exploration. We should point out one caution: having the same career style as that of a specific job doesn't mean that you would enjoy that job or even be good at it; it simply means that people in that job tend to resemble you, personality-wise. In addition to personality, an individual's educational

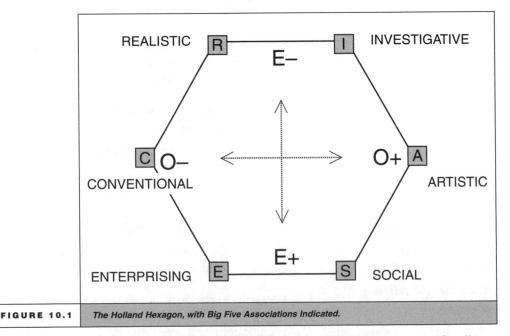

| FIGURE 10.1 | *The Holland Hexagon, with Big Five Associations Indicated.* |

Source: Adapted from J. L. Holland, "Exploring Careers with a Typology: What We Have Learned and Some New Directions," *American Psychologist*, 1996, *51*(4) 397–406.

level, background experiences, value systems, personal needs, and sheer intelligence all contribute to whether she or he enjoys and excels at a particular job. Holland, incidentally, is not the only researcher who has attempted to define the major career styles. A more recent effort is that of Edgar Schein (1993) and his Career Anchors model.

Rules and Exceptions

We find value in such career exploration aids as those developed by Holland and Schein. However, the Big Five represents a much more precise vocabulary for describing an individual's career style. Each region of the Big Five dimensions suggests a variety of different types of careers that might be associated with it. Table 10.1 illustrates the robustness of the Five-Factor Model for explaining the relationship of career to personality.

By looking at the combination of an individual's more salient and midrange traits, we are able to align that person more precisely with specific job titles. One such commercial venture is at the website www.discoverme.com, which administers the Big Five on-line and instantly compares an individual's profile to its bank of job profiles. Candidates who fit a company's profile for a particular job are notified and their name and profile are submitted to the company.

Big Five job profiles are full of rules and exceptions. For example, we mentioned in Chapter Eight that the ideal leader profile is E+. This is the rule. One exception would be a manager of research and development. R&D staff are typically highly introverted, and the daily dose of a garrulous manager might be more than they could stomach, preferring instead an E= manager who can turn on the charm around higher-up decision makers and external funding sources, yet chill out around the scientists' lair. On occasion even a rather stable job, one that seldom varies from company to company, might have dramatic exceptions. Take the job of logger. For the most part, the logger's job is to cut trees. This would be true in Oregon and Alberta, but in Nevada the logger would also have to find trees! Similarly, some managers have responsibility for strategic planning while others don't.

We list a variety of ideal job profiles in Table 10.2. Look at them as the rule, but be aware that many exceptions and variations exist. Think of them as a point of departure, a beginning place for dialogue about a particular job. Organizational culture, unique market

TABLE 10.1	*Examples of Jobs and Careers at Each Level of the Big Five Dimensions.*		
	−	**=**	**+**
N	Pilot; surgeon; leader; sales representative; manager; police officer	Facilitator; consultant; interviewer	Customer service representative; social worker; participant in contact sports; flight attendant; teacher
E	Researcher; information technology worker; accountant; bookkeeper; engineer; writer; patent lawyer; service worker; lab technician; clerical worker; data entry specialist; football free safety	Teacher; consultant; facilitator; estate lawyer; interviewer; receptionist	Sales representative; leader; litigator; entertainer; manager; product demonstrator; hotel concierge
O	Pilot; technician; repair and maintenance worker; health care specialist (for example, orthopedic hand specialist); manager; art reproduction technician; performing artist; football interior lineman; data entry specialist; clerical worker; tactician	Facilitator; interviewer; middle manager with a blend of tactical and strategic responsibilities	Visionary leader; tax accountant; marketing specialist; advertising executive; consultant; health care generalist (for example, orthopedic generalist); artist, composer, or designer; football quarterback; basketball point guard; strategist
A	Entrepreneur; litigator; manager; leader; real estate developer; police officer	Facilitator; arbitrator; interviewer	Service worker; social worker; customer service representative; law professor; receptionist
C	Maintenance worker; troubleshooter; person in a staff (versus line) position	Facilitator; interviewer; manager who wishes to have a personal life	Leader; person in a line position (manager, supervisor); sales representative; proofreader

Job or Role	N	E	O	A	C
			Big Five Profiles Associated with Common Jobs.	**TABLE 10.2**	
Antiterrorist operative	–	+			+
Architect	–	=	++	–	+
Attila the Hun type of leader	+	–	–	–	+
Autocrat (decision-making style)	+		–	–	+
Bomb disposal expert	–	=			+
Branch manager	–	–	=	=	
Bureaucrat (decision-making style)	–				+
Catalyst/team builder type of leader	–	+	+	+	+
Combat fighter pilot	–	+	+		++
Consensus builder (decision-making style)	=	+		+	=
Consultant	=	=	+	=	=
Customer service representative	=+	+		=	
Diplomat (decision-making style)	–			=	–
Entrepreneur		+	+	–	+
Facilitator	=	=	=	=	=
Flight attendant	+	+	+		
Hotel service worker		–		+	+
Laissez-faire type of leader	=	=	=	+	–
Leader (generic)	–	+	+	–	+
Machine operator		–	–		+
Manager (generic)	–	+	–	–	+
Manufacturing manager	–	=	=	=	+
Night shift worker	–	–		–	
Participative type of leader	=	+	=	=	+
Physician, primary care	–	=		=	–
Project manager	=	+	=	–	+
Research and development specialist	–		I	=	
Salesperson	–	++		–	+
Solo circumnavigator of the world	–	–	=	–	++
Teller	=	=	–		+
Trainer	=+	+	=	+	=
Troubleshooter type of leader	–	=	–	–	–
Visionary type of leader	–	+	+	–	+

Key: ++: Very high score (above 65); +: Moderately high score (56–65); =: Midrange score (45–55); –: Moderately low score (35–44); ––: Very low score (below 35). Two symbols (for example, =+): Wider range associated with the job or role.

segments, national differences, corporate goals, and many other circumstances can modify the kind of personality that is ideally suited for a particular job. A sales job in the United States typically requires an A– personality, but many Canadian and Asian markets respond far better to A+ salespeople. However, a Canadian or Asian sales force comprised of A+ salespeople might want to consider hiring a handful of A– salespeople for assignment to markets like that of the United States. Note that in Table 10.2, not all columns have entries for each row. When a column is empty, you can conclude either that the dimension is irrelevant to the job or role under consideration or that it can vary depending on the specific circumstances surrounding the job.

Let's now take a look at two career stars—people who have the Big Five profile that is typically associated with high performance in their field—and one professional who does not.

Career Case Study 1
"Super Narc"

Let's start with "Super Narc," who has been ranked among the top five agents in the U.S. Drug Enforcement Agency in arrests for drug trafficking along the southern U.S. border. Super Narc's Big Five profile is presented in Figure 10.2. Look first at the Five-Factor scores at the top of the figure. Super Narc's salient factors are very low A and high C. Here's a law enforcement agent who is disciplined and ambitious (C+) and who takes nothing from anyone (A– –). He's responsive, either calm or excitable as needed (N=); is comfortable both around people and alone (E=); and possesses a balance of imagination and efficiency (O=).

Although these facets provide an excellent infrastructure for a narcotics agent, they are even more telling and foundational for the type of border duty he performs. His very high score on intensity (N2 = 67) reveals a man with an angry edge who seldom loses his intensity of pursuit. His very low score on rebound time (N4 = 32) reveals a man who wastes no time licking his wounds and rebounds quickly from failure, disappointment, or crisis. He has a very low need for companionship, as shown by his scores on enthusiasm (E1 = 28) and sociability (E2 = 39), and is comfortable on stakeouts and other solitary pursuits. He never minces words (A4 = 28) and requires no outside leadership or crutches (E4 = 70). He is not often bored (O2 = 40) and focuses easily on the here-and-now and on details (O4 = 42). He trusts practically no one (E5 = 33), wastes no energy trying to be nice (E6 = 22), seldom if ever backs down in a conflict (A2 = 28), and enjoys winning and getting credit (A3 = 29). He has an unlimited drive and will to achieve (C3 = 71) and enough caution to avoid stupid mistakes (C5 = 59). A better foundation could not be laid for such a job.

Career Case Study 2
The Arch Architect

From our star-studded gallery of successful profiles we draw now from the ranks of high-achieving CEOs. A late-middle-aged architect turned her local firm of 40 architects and engineers into a regional one of some 150 in a period of around four years. Growth, profitability, and a corral full of happy campers characterized this enterprise before, during, and after this spurt. To help explain her apparent ease in taking her firm to the next level, we must acknowledge that she had previously demonstrated high ability as both an architect and a leader of architects through her experience with another regional, noncompeting firm. But past successes aside, look at the personality infrastructure from which she has launched her successes

	0	45	55	100
N			49	
E			45	
O			48	
A	21			
C				61
N1: Sensitiveness			53	
N2: Intensity				67
N3: Interpretation			51	
N4: Rebound Time	32			
E1: Enthusiasm	28			
E2: Sociability	39			
E3: Energy Mode	42			
E4: Taking Charge				70
E5: Trust in Others	33			
E6: Tact	22			
O1: Imagination		47		
O2: Complexity	40			
O3: Change			52	
O4: Scope	42			
A1: Service			54	
A2: Agreement	28			
A3: Deference	29			
A4: Reserve	28			
A5: Reticence		45		
C1: Perfectionism			52	
C2: Organization			55	
C3: Drive				71
C4: Concentration	41			
C5: Methodicalness			59	
	0	45	55	100

"Super Narc."	**FIGURE 10.2**

	0	45	55	100
N	40			
E			59	
O				75
A		44		
C				73
N1: Sensitiveness		43		
N2: Intensity		41		
N3: Interpretation	33			
N4: Rebound Time	32			
E1: Enthusiasm				64
E2: Sociability			56	
E3: Energy Mode			59	
E4: Taking Charge			56	
E5: Trust in Others		40		
E6: Tact			52	
O1: Imagination				75
O2: Complexity				80
O3: Change				73
O4: Scope			56	
A1: Service		43		
A2: Agreement			45	
A3: Deference		38		
A4: Reserve		35		
A5: Reticence		36		
C1: Perfectionism				64
C2: Organization				68
C3: Drive				81
C4: Concentration				72
C5: Methodicalness				74
	0	45	55	100

FIGURE 10.3 *The Arch Architect.*

(see Figure 10.3). Her five factors each meet or exceed the ideal leader profile portrayed in Figure 8.1, with excesses in O and C. For architecture, being O++ is not only understandable, but desirable. In order to become successful, an architect must have O+'s imagination and comfort with complexity, and a manager of architects must be able to relate to the highly imaginative professionals in his or her charge. This architect's C++ profile (73) points to the drive and discipline that was necessary to triple the size of the practice.

Specific facets account for the natural fit between the architect and her role. She approaches her tasks with optimism (N3 = 33), so important for her role as the primary salesperson. She shows no reluctance to be the out-front person (A5 = 36), unlike many other architects who are more private and self-conscious. Her very low rebound time (N4 = 32) enables her to avoid losing time and opportunities, since she has no need to recover after losing a bid, yet she has just enough of a nervous edge (N1 = 43) and emotional intensity (N2 = 41) to propel her drive with an ever-present appetite for acquisition and challenge.

Her high enthusiasm (E1 = 64) facilitates the development and maintenance of relationships with clients, vendors, and associates, while her moderate sociability and energy (E2 = 56; E3 = 59) render her comfortable in her meeting and greeting role, yet also comfortable taking the private time to study the numbers and the details of the business. Her forceful leadership is supported by her expressiveness (A4 = 35), which suggests that people around her seldom have to read her mind, yet her moderate tendency to take charge (E4 = 56) allows her to delegate broad authority to her studio heads and encourage a participative, highly motivating team approach to management.

Her O facets are all very high, which is to be expected of an excellent architect. The exception is scope (O4 = 56), which is sufficiently moderate for her to be comfortable with the big picture, yet willing to plunge into the details (where, after all, God resides!). Her low (but not too low) trust of others (E5 = 40) and service orientation (A1 = 43) prevent her from being duped by any of her stakeholders and are a major reason for her consistent record of profitability. She shows a moderate tendency toward toughness, yet is able to be tender. Expressed another way, appropriate trust, so mandatory in relationships, must be balanced with appropriate skepticism. This manager has the necessary skepticism, yet not to the exclusion of having the necessary trust, which would likely be the case if her score were some twenty points lower on E5. Her moderate tact (E6 = 52) and agreement (A2 = 45) support her role as a negotiator and deal maker, in which she must constantly pursue win-win situations for her clients and associates. Seldom a submitter and seldom defiant, she is always fair. Her low deference score (A3 = 38) fuels her drive with a need for recognition and honors, evidenced by the accumulation of publications and awards she and her associates have amassed. All five C facets are very high, which would be expected of someone who is both ambitious and able to provide the necessary discipline for her dreams.

Career Case Study 3
The Penitent Litigator

Over the years, we've often been called on to help professionals in some kind of crisis. Either their boss or associates call us to "fix" these professionals or they call us themselves, in a desire to feel better about their careers. Let's take a look at one of these repair efforts.

Once there was a frazzled attorney who was highly successful and wealthy, yet miserable in her work. A litigating lawyer in a firm of some fifty professionals, this woman went home every evening wishing she could start life over. Why? A look at the Five-Factor profile in Figure 10.4 provides two major clues.

	0	45	55	100
N	40			
E	38			
O				72
A				64
C				62
N1: Sensitiveness		47		
N2: Intensity	32			
N3: Interpretation	42			
N4: Rebound Time		54		
E1: Enthusiasm			57	
E2: Sociability	34			
E3: Energy Mode	41			
E4: Taking Charge	36			
E5: Trust in Others				64
E6: Tact				70
O1: Imagination				74
O2: Complexity				65
O3: Change				69
O4: Scope				75
A1: Service				68
A2: Agreement		49		
A3: Deference				74
A4: Reserve		48		
A5: Reticence	38			
C1: Perfectionism				65
C2: Organization				71
C3: Drive			56	
C4: Concentration				74
C5: Methodicalness		68		
	0	45	55	100

FIGURE 10.4 *The Penitent Litigator.*

First, this lawyer's E score is 38, and courtroom litigation is a tough life for an Introvert. With the constant need to be in the thick of the action—listening, interacting, strategizing—even more extraverted lawyers will find that this way of life takes its toll on them. An E– lawyer would be more likely to find joy in doing research, writing briefs, and having minimal to moderate contact with other associates in meetings and conferences—for example, as a copyright and patent attorney. Second, litigating attorneys don't have the reputation of being nice guys, but this litigator's A score is 64! Peaceful, humble, and altruistic—not in my courtroom! Here's a litigator who's expected to go into the courtroom every day with a killer instinct, yet who has the meekness of a lamb. We're reminded of a needlepoint we saw in a Gaithersburg, Maryland, savings and loan office: "And the lion and the lamb shall lie together, and the lamb shall not get much sleep." Well, this lamb was certainly leery of the lair!

Her facets give us more detail about her discontent. She's a generally calm person (N2 = 32), which suggests that she may have difficulty finding the intensity, the flame of anger, necessary to do battle in the throes of litigation. On the other hand, her borderline high requirement for rebound time (N4 = 54) indicates that she needs some time to recover from setbacks and losses. Although she's warm and likable (E1 = 57), she likes her privacy (E2 = 34), something that's rare in the life of the litigator. And her low energy mode (E3 = 41) and distaste for taking charge (E4 = 36) suggest that she'd prefer something more sedentary and laid-back than litigation.

All of her O scores are very high, which is what drew her to litigation in the first place. No two days are the same, and wildly different cases create a broad-ranging set of demands for developing instant expertise. But she's meek—not a wimp, but meek. Taking on the role of bad guy and litigator, while gilding the future, tarnishes the soul of the high A. A moderate agreement score (A2 = 49) does support her need to be a good negotiator, but is that litigation? We think not. A score of 49 would be good for an arbitrator or judge, but something along the line of a 15 or 20 would be better for a litigator, who must go for the jugular and take no prisoners. And look at the high C scores. Surely the spontaneous, freewheeling life of the litigator, who must be prepared to switch tracks at a moment's notice when the prosecution tries a surprise tactic, must be less than satisfying for someone so orderly, disciplined, and focused.

After one career counseling session, this talented but unhappy attorney realized that although she could perform at a high level as a litigator, litigation was not a natural fit with her trait infrastructure. She determined then and there to seek a teaching position in a law school. We heard back from her a year later. She had taken a position teaching agricultural law (a special fondness of hers) at a reputable law school, had started a new journal devoted to articles on agricultural law, and was happy. Her trait infrastructure finally supported a compatible career.

The last several chapters have focused on individual profiles. The next two will concentrate on two or more profiles at a time: partnerships and teams.

11

One-on-One

Troubleshooting Partnerships and Relationships

> **What is a friend? A single soul dwelling in two bodies.**
>
> —*Aristotle,* Lives of Eminent Philosophers

More than two millennia in our past, Aristotle said what contemporary research has confirmed. Over the long haul, the more similar two individuals are, the more satisfying the relationship. In a 1989 "B.C." comic strip, a bold ant sings from the top of his anthill, "I gotta be meee!" No sooner is the lyric sung than the ant is zapped off the top of his hill by the anteater, who laments unapologetically, "Unfortunately, so do I." Clearly, according to Aristotle, these two could never be friends, because they don't share the same soul, the same "rock bottom," the same trait infrastructure.

Two relatively recent studies of interpersonal relationships have clarified the importance of trait similarity to satisfaction in relationships. Burgoon, Stern, and Dillman (1995, pp. 117 ff.) emphasize the beneficial effects of similarity between two partners. They find that partners who begin on a positive footing actually become more like each other. The traits converge, as it were. They call this process "reciprocity." Partners who start off more shakily, and who in fact are relatively more different than similar, undergo a process they label "compensation," in which the partners change away from each other. The traits diverge, moving even farther apart. Other research confirms that although opposites seem more appealing in the short term, both in business and in romance, being with people with similar profiles is more satisfying over the long haul.

Kiesler (1996, p. 6) emphasizes the importance of what he calls "behavior concordance": "Any interpersonal act is designed to elicit from a respondent reactions that confirm, reinforce, or validate the actor's self-presentation and that make it more likely that the actor will continue to emit similar interpersonal acts." In other words, the anteater didn't validate the ant! Kiesler is trying to say that when we behave a certain way in the presence of our partner, we expect our partner to react in a way that's accepting of us as an individual. If we see a news story about our partner's schoolchild, clip it, and present it to her at work, we certainly don't expect her to say, "Don't you have something better to do with your time?" or "No thanks, I've already got two dozen of those things." Kiesler goes on to conclude that when behavior is concordant, when my behavior gets an accepting and validating response from you, the chances of satisfaction in the relationship are high. He further points out that the likelihood of such concordant behavior is highest when two partners are similar with respect to their trait infrastructure (as well as having similar intelligence and physical characteristics). In addition to such concordant behavior, similarity of traits also encourages reciprocal behavior, which involves responding in kind. I ask you out to lunch today, and tomorrow you ask me. Such reciprocity is another way of validating or accepting a person's value as an individual.

We are going to be most satisfied when we can be ourselves and don't have to put on an act. Kiesler observes that midrange people, whose traits are more moderate, act like universal donors, able to be satisfied with the widest possible range of partners. For example, an ambiverted team member can be comfortable around both more introverted associates and more extraverted ones. However, people with extreme traits, like those with Big Five scores above 65 (the upper 7 percent of the population) or below 35 (the lower 7 percent), are more likely to be unsatisfied with people at the other end of the continuum. We both score very high in O and find people who are low in O difficult to enjoy; in turn, they find us tedious or tiring because of our multiplicity of interests. On the other hand, we're both close to midrange in the other four dimensions and are able to relate satisfactorily with many people on those terms.

Neil Diamond sang, "You don't send me flowers anymore." The subtext of that lyric is: "My behavior doesn't elicit from you the validating behaviors it used to." Whether people are in a marriage, a business partnership, a boss-subordinate relationship, a relationship between two work associates, or a corporate or team culture, they prefer a context in which they can behave naturally. Introverts want to introvert, Challengers want to challenge, and "trusters" want to be able to trust. Anything different is unsatisfying.

Dag Hammarskjöld is credited with once suggesting that world peace might result if each of us could establish just one healthy relationship with another person. Sometimes the going is difficult, in spite of our similarities and often because of our differences. In Chapter Nine, we looked at ways to establish rapport with people whose traits differed from ours (see Table 9.2). Nothing, however, is as powerful in sustaining relationships as accepting others for who they are. This is easier when we are similar, but nobler when we are different.

Partnership Case Study 1
Two Plant Managers in Conflict

Several years back, two plant managers, who managed two different manufacturing processes under one roof, were at each other's throats, and we were called in to do some peacemaking. After they had completed a brief Big Five profile (see the results in Figure 11.1), we asked them to identify the

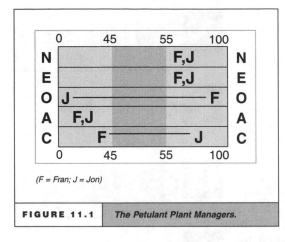

(F = Fran; J = Jon)

FIGURE 11.1 *The Petulant Plant Managers.*

issues that divided them. That was easy, they said. Fran accused Jon of sacrificing future growth potential by emphasizing short-term profits. Jon accused Fran of spending money on process improvements at the cost of profitability goals. Jon said, "My side of the plant has to tighten its belt because of your side's self-indulgence." Fran retorted, "My side is worrying about whether it will have jobs in ten years because you're milking your process dry and not preparing for the next generation of technology."

We then drew their attention to their profiles. The glaring differences were in O and C. Fran was the futuristic idea generator, comfortable with change and a philosophy of continuing improvement (O+) but undisciplined in managing to the bottom line (C–). Jon was the conservative efficiency expert who steadfastly defended the status quo (O–) and was so focused on his immediate goals that he resisted any distractions (C+). We pointed out that as a team, they made an ideal partnership. Fran brought strategy and Jon brought tactics. Without both of them, the plant was doomed, but if they could each appreciate what the other brought to the table, they would prevail. Both were needed to win the war. They saw the light and agreed to meet on a regular basis to offer a counterbalance to each other's decision making. Fran would force Jon to consider his options, and Jon would force Fran to prioritize her wish list. Together, they could blend dreams and realities into steady growth.

Partnership Case Study 2
Two Bank Managers in the Middle

Over a twelve-month period, we had the opportunity to work extensively with approximately sixty middle managers in a division of a major financial institution. Several teams were functioning at this level in the company, and two of those teams had to work together cooperatively on a daily basis, in spite of having different goals and mandates, in order to accomplish the overall goals for their division, which was geographically dispersed over a multistate region.

Having conducted team-building sessions for both of these teams, we knew the teams and their managers well. During both of their Big Five team-building sessions, comments, questions, and discussions about work and process difficulties with the other team surfaced frequently. In a follow-up discussion with the managers of the two teams, we suggested that they consider having both teams participate in a single team-building session, where the members of each team could learn about the personalities of the people on the other team while working out their operational difficulties. The team managers thought that this was a great idea and began planning the event.

One of the issues to be decided in planning the event was how the managers could best introduce the session and convey to the team members that they had accepted the value of the Big Five and wanted their teams to use what they'd learned about it, both within each team and in communicating with the other team. The idea we finally settled on was to separate the whole group into the five levels for each of the Big Five traits (very high, high, and so forth). Prior to the group's performing this activity, however, the two managers would perform it as an example (see Figure 11.2).

Here are a few of the examples the two managers discussed from their various positions on the five levels. We haven't included the specific nature of the managers' work in order to protect their identities as well as that of their company. As you read these examples, please keep in mind that the two managers, X and Y, were making a strong effort to be as humorous as possible during this opening introduction

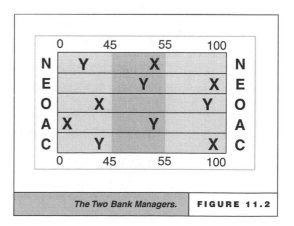

The Two Bank Managers. **FIGURE 11.2**

in order to encourage their teams to be honest in openly confronting the issues that divided them. Throughout the comments reported below, their teams sprinkled the pauses with chuckles, grins, and outright laughter. The managers had extensively planned all their comments together with us ahead of time in an effort to highlight some of their stronger differences. They both said privately later that they found the exercise of preparing the presentation and comparing their personalities to be fun and extremely valuable to their working relationship.

N Scale

Manager X (N=)

"I take matters more seriously and personally than Y does, especially when the matters concern our internal customers."

"I know I worry more than she does, and I worry about whether her team can get different tasks done."

"I anticipate likely problems in our process or within the division more readily than she does."

"I wish I were as calm during a crisis as she is. I've got to get some of that liquid ice for my veins!"

Manager Y (N–)

"I'm definitely more laid back than X is." (chuckles from the team members as she collapses onto the conference table) "Someone asked me once if I had a pulse."

"I know we'll eventually get around to the needs of our internal customers as soon as we solve other difficulties."

"I usually don't worry whether X or his team will get their work done; I don't even worry about my team. Maybe I should!"

"I know if I let X vent his frustrations first, we'll then be able to rationally solve the problem, but if I move immediately into problem solving, he won't let me go there until all the frustration comes out."

E Scale

Manager X (E++)

"Well, as you can all attest, there are absolutely no problems getting me to speak out in a meeting."

"You'll also notice that I often party until the very end on our evenings out during the regional meetings. I don't recall that Y has ever been in the last cab back to the hotel with me!"

"I have to talk things through in order to think; sometimes people in the offices next to mine think I'm talking to them when I'm simply talking aloud to myself about what I'm going to do next."

"I really need face-to-face contact with my team. I suspect my team gets tired of my three-times-a-week team conference calls."

Manager Y (E=)

"Now let's see who stays awake after lunch better today, since I'm sure I got more sleep than X did last night with my earlier cab ride."

"I enjoy our regional meetings, but I have to have some down time away from you guys. I just can't go from seven in the morning until midnight for three straight days. Otherwise, I'd turn into a zombie." (knowing smiles and nods from the Ambiverts in the room)

"I'm comfortable leading a discussion, and I'm comfortable letting some others on the team take the leadership role, especially X."

"I find our quarterly face-to-face meetings adequate. I think we get along fine with our weekly conference call and with e-mail."

O Scale

Manager X (O–)

"I'm a great tactical planner. I make sure that every detail is handled in our plan. I'm not sure Y knows what details are."

"I know that if I have to come up with a new product or service, I can't do it without her off-the-wall ideas."

"I'm really good at managing budgets and cost containment. Just ask my team's slapped hands."

"One of my personal struggles is wanting to meet face-to-face with people because of my E+, but knowing that I won't let myself spend the money to do it because of my O– budget priorities."

Manager Y (O++)

"I have to have a lot of variety in my job or I get antsy and start looking for new projects, and my team truly dreads that!"

"I think I do my best work when I'm thinking and planning strategically for our company's future. That really gets my mind going."

"I wish I were as good at cost containment as X is. Keeping us within budget with all my wild ideas is almost painful at times."

A Scale

Manager X (A– –)

"On any topic, I'm right; Y is wrong; end of story."

"On any topic, I'm right; my team is wrong; end of story."

"On any topic, my team is right; Y's team is wrong; end of story."

"If you won't give me a good argument for what you want to do, I'll refuse you because I won't respect you for not standing up for yourself."

"Seriously, I'm trying to learn that there are other points of view besides mine with legitimate reasons for the views. Gosh, that was hard to admit to!"

Manager Y (A=)

"I know that on any topic, X is right and I'm wrong; end of story."

"I know that on any topic, I'm right and my team is wrong, because I like to win sometimes!"

"I'm approachable. I don't always have to be right, and I think I appreciate other points of view fairly well."

"I like to stand up for the person who gets run over by X, even if that person is on his team."

C Scale

Manager X (C++)

"You think I haven't heard all of your under-the-breath comments when you call me anal-retentive, but I have," (dramatic pause) *"and I am!"* (much loud laughter from both teams)

"I want everyone in this room, especially Y, to begin responding to my voice-mail messages immediately—not an hour from now, not tomorrow, not next week. My priorities are always more important than your priorities. It says so in the company handbook!"

"I wish all of you were as organized as I am. You too could have a clean desk at the end of the day, without sweeping it all into your top drawer."

"One of the things I value in Y is her multitasking. It drives me bonkers to have to stop working on one of my top priorities to deal with something else I hadn't planned to do."

"Some of you are chocoholics, some of you are foodaholics, so by now you should know that I'm a workaholic."

"You should also know that I'm trying to be more flexible. In fact, I scheduled an hour of flexibility in my Day Planner last week!"

Manager Y (C–)

"Well, my C score is just barely into the low range with a 44, but I seem like the poster child for flexibility and spontaneity compared to X."

"I do like to make decisions in this lifetime rather than studying all the details for what seems like decades before deciding, the way he does."

"And I will admit that I haven't had to visit 'Workaholics Anonymous' recently. I strive for more balance in my life."

"I admit it, I really do envy X's organizational skills and neatness."

"And, as our final item, I'm really pleased to report that the anal-retentive label has never been applied to me at any time!"

These two managers effectively broke the ice between their two teams for the team-building session that followed their hilarious Big Five introduction. By poking fun at themselves and using real examples from their work, they set up some very candid discussions as the members of the two teams divided into the five levels for each factor. The exercise in understanding personality, in turn, led to a very helpful problem-solving session about operational issues between the two teams.

Who said teamwork has to be dull? Not the Big Five!

Often, partnerships fail because they start off on the wrong foot, perhaps because of some misguided gimmick like the television fiasco, "So You Want to Marry a Millionaire." From partnerships of two, we now progress to looking at the ways in which individual differences in trait infrastructures can work both magic and doom in work teams. Whereas partnerships usually benefit from similarity, or homogeneity, of profiles, Chapter Twelve will show how teams typically benefit from diversity, or heterogeneity, of profiles.

12

Team Development

Roles, Phases, Needs, and All That

Just a few years ago, it seems, when someone used the word *team* in a workplace conversation, most of us thought immediately of a sports team or perhaps even a team of horses, rather than a work team. As the idea of teams came into vogue in the workplace, we weren't sure if we wanted to be on one or not. Today, teams are no longer a novelty or an optional pastime; they're an integral part of the way most of our organizations get work done.

Because of the extensive use of teams, some organizations have rightly or wrongly assumed that people now innately know how to work in teams, and that by simply being put together, they'll "be" a team. Meanwhile, many people find themselves thrown together with co-workers they have viewed as incompetent, in pursuit of a loosely defined goal; these people may have a less than satisfying experience with teaming.

One rather progressive manufacturing manager with whom we had worked during a leadership program invited us into his company to work with a relatively new team that was already operating. His idea was that we would tell the team about all the opportunities they would have with the Big Five and that they would, as a team, decide to use the model. We delivered the following presentation to them.

Reasons to Use the Big Five Model with Teams

1. *It provides a common vocabulary to discuss individual differences:* Using consistent terms to describe personality differences is equivalent to using consistent terms to describe an interoffice memo form (as in "the routing slip"), a departmental report (as in "the weekly inventory report"), or a manufacturing part (as in "quarter-inch aluminum pipe"). We all know what we mean by these terms, and that knowledge helps overall communication in our organizations.

2. *It helps individual team members to understand themselves better:* From the very beginning, we need to start with ourselves. Unless we understand what stresses us, stimulates us, interests us, motivates us, or distracts us, we can't know who we really are and how we relate to other people.

3. *It gives each team member more understanding of the others on the team:* As long as we're thinking, "I'm right and the rest of you bozos are wrong," our teams will not achieve teamwork. Only when we can explain our views as "different" instead of "right" or "wrong" can we hope to form teams of people who will work together effectively.

4. *It provides teams with explanations for their group dynamics and behaviors:* Teams wonder why they work differently from other teams they hear about (for example, "We all try to talk at once without listening to each other [E+]," or "We have a difficult time trying to think of new products [O–]"). The Big Five can help to explain the reasons for these dynamics and behaviors.

5. *It assists teams in planning strategies for capitalizing on strengths and minimizing weaker areas:* The "develop," "support," and "compensate" strategies of Chapter Sixteen apply as well to teams as they do to individuals.

Ways to Use the Big Five with Teams

1. *For individual feedback sessions:* A trained consultant can provide invaluable feedback about what one's Big Five scores mean in a workplace setting. Often, relating scores to individuals prior to a team-building session helps them to accept the learning that will take place. Also, people sometimes distrust personality instruments, especially if one has been poorly used or misapplied in the past. Hearing about the results before a group session takes place can make some people (especially N+ people) more comfortable with the Big Five outcomes and the way the model is going to be applied to the team.

2. *In team-building sessions with exercises:* Exercises can foster discussion in a nonthreatening way about what may or may not be occurring within the team.

3. *For open sharing of scores among team members:* When a team takes a Big Five instrument with the idea of using it for a team session, ethically, team members need to be advised that they'll be expected to share their scores with others. The scores can then confirm and help explain behaviors that others may have observed about a team member.

4. *For 360° feedback about the way an individual is perceived by the other team members:* It occasionally happens that a particular team member's self-perception is completely different from the way others perceive his or her work on the team. Candid 360° feedback can often wake up a poor performer or team member to the reality of workplace expectations.

5. *In establishing personal and team areas that may need improvement:* What if the team is made up of people who score C– and are continually late with deadlines? The Big Five can be used to develop compensating strategies (see Chapter Sixteen).

6. *To give Big Five feedback to the team about meetings:* For example, are the E+ members dominating the discussions or talking during the meetings? If so, the Big Five traits can be used to explain to the team how this helps or hinders them in accomplishing their objectives.

7. *For locating additional team members to provide new perspectives, ideas, and personality diversity:* We have long contended that personality is another strong element of diversity that should be acknowledged in the workplace. Other points of view may help teams make better-quality decisions than if the team members all have the same personality characteristics. However, personality diversity usually means more potential conflict that must be anticipated before the team goes to work, so that team members can plan ahead of time how to manage it.

8. *In identifying the needs or styles of others outside the team:* An understanding of personalities outside the team may give the team members insights into the best way to make presentations to their manager or influence other teams they have to work with in the company. This could be a distinct advantage for the team in securing the resources it needs, having its projects approved, and receiving appropriate recognition for its hard work, among other benefits.

Once a team has used an instrument to measure its team members' scores on the Big Five model, there are several ways to develop the knowledge that the Big Five can provide to the team. One way is to use a large graph of the team, such as the color foldout graph on this book's back cover (available for teams in poster size from the *Cent*ACS catalog and website). As the team members examine the graph where all their scores are placed, they should answer the following questions:

1. Are our scores fairly evenly distributed along the scales or do they cluster in particular areas?

2. As a group, which traits seem to be dominant or have more clusters?

3. What strengths could these clusters indicate for our team interactions, our work processes, or our team meetings?

4. What potential weaknesses could those clusters indicate for our team interactions, our work processes, or our team meetings?

5. Over what issues or in what situations could we potentially experience conflicts?

6. Which members of our team could potentially feel left out or excluded from our interactions unless we pay close attention to their points of view?

7. Which team members might be natural leaders or facilitators? (Do you remember our discussions about this in Chapters Eight and Nine?)

8. Which team members should we look to for troubleshooting or trust building?

We find that most team members can readily discuss these questions once they understand what the basic personality traits mean. Then, as problems arise within the team, they can revisit questions 4 through 8 to create new strategies for dealing with the problems that personality issues or assigned team roles may potentially cause within the team.

> *"A team of two like-minded people is likely overstaffed."*
> —Jon Younger,
> Managing Director,
> Novations Group, Inc.

Team Case Study
The Lab Technicians

In the course of our consulting work, we were invited to work with a very conflicted team of ten lab technicians who were particularly memorable. These people worked in a small research and development division of forty people within a global manufacturing company. As the situation unfolded, we found that a new department manager, who was thought to be very progressive in his thinking and willingness to try new techniques, had told these ten technicians that they would work together as a team, although they were not given any type of meeting training or preparation.

The previous manager of the department had micromanaged everyone, was very controlling, and had created clear distinctions between the "professional" staff—the chemists and engineers with doctorate degrees—and the technicians who ran the scientists' lab experiments, most of whom had no college degrees. The conflict came about when the ten technicians were told to form a team and start holding meetings. Their team assignment from the new department manager was to redesign their existing technician's career development plan, an undertaking that none of them had any inkling how to do.

The technicians had started meeting once a month for an hour to work on their team assignment. The new manager had generously provided food for the early morning meetings, so everyone showed up, but other than eating, they didn't know how to proceed. After their first four meetings they had reached a stalemate: five members of the team wanted computer training and five did not. They hit a verbal roadblock and couldn't get around it because they had no knowledge or experience from which to draw, yet they dutifully continued to go to the monthly meeting. Their lack of agreement and opposite positions in the team meeting were beginning to affect their daily communication and work relationships within the department.

At this point, we were called in to help. The department manager asked the consultant to attend the team's upcoming meeting and informed the team that she'd be there. The consultant arrived first but didn't select a place to sit until she could observe the team members. As they entered, they deferentially spoke to the consultant, picked up their breakfast, and selected their seats at the long conference room table, five sitting at one end and five at the other. After introducing herself, the consultant sat alone in the middle area. Trying to speak inclusively to both ends of the table and rotating her head from one end of the table to the other as if she were at a tennis match, she said that she knew they were having some disagreements as a team, but she was not there to tell them what to do. Judging by their body language, this seemed to put them at ease. Rather than starting with their disagreement, the consultant told them that she'd like to get some background information about what had led up to the current situation.

That was all it took to get them started. For the next hour, the consultant heard from each of the ten people in the room about such issues as the unkindness of their old manager, their uncertainty about their new manager, their frustration at being told to do something they thought the human resources department should be doing for them, the difficulty of not knowing where to begin or how to conduct a meeting properly, their fear that they'd be fired for not accomplishing their task at the team meetings, their uncertainty about how to get over their team disagreements, and so forth for twelve full flipchart pages of small print. As we had suspected from the original phone call, we'd landed in the middle of an unplanned change management process fostered by a well-intentioned manager.

The consultant then introduced a process to help them prioritize the team's key issues so that she could begin to help them make some headway among themselves and with management. Once they felt that their big problems were at least manageable, if not yet resolved, the team was ready to move forward by taking a good look at themselves. You've no doubt guessed what tool we used: we gave each team member the Big Five assessment. The results are given in Figure 12.1.

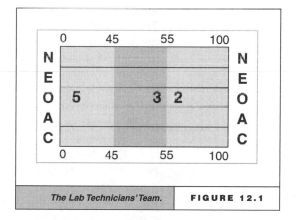

The Lab Technicians' Team. **FIGURE 12.1**

The dimension where the team members had the most unusual profile was the O scale. Five members were clustered around 30 on the scale as O−− and five were clustered around 55 (three just below 55 and two just above). These scores explained a great deal and began to help the team members understand why they sat at opposite ends of the table.

The O−− members insisted that they didn't want their jobs to change to include computer training; they didn't even want to learn to turn on a computer. They knew everything there was to know about their jobs and were completely content with the way they'd been done for the last twenty-five years. Taking time out for training was just another way to goof off from the "real work" they needed to accomplish during their workday and a waste of the company's good money, which could be better spent by increasing the technicians' paychecks. The O−− members were confident that their proven method of recording the lab data each day with paper and pen didn't need improvement. It was accurate and precise, and it couldn't be lost in cyberspace when a computer bombed. They didn't want to have to learn new skills; to their way of thinking, it was up to the chemists and engineers to analyze the data from the lab experiments. Data analysis didn't belong in the technicians' job description. As they pointed out strongly, "That's why the Ph.D.'s are paid the big bucks by the company."

Meanwhile, the O= and O+ members, who were more open to the change the new manager was bringing to the department, wanted to broaden their existing, routine jobs with more responsibility and different kinds of activities. Given their tendency to look farther into the future, they also viewed computer and software training as a way to acquire new skills that would give them better job security in what was becoming a more volatile job market. They thought that knowing how to do more kinds of tasks and procedures in the workplace would make it easier for them to get jobs at other companies if their division should disappear through a merger or acquisition (not an uncommon event in this company). Computer and software training, to them, was job enrichment and made them more valuable to their company, especially if they could learn how to analyze and summarize data for the chemists and engineers.

Clearly, this was a difficult situation for the team as its members staked themselves out self-righteously on extreme positions. It took time to overcome the conflict, and the Big Five vocabulary was the key. Once the team members understood their own personality tendencies and positions, they could begin to understand and ultimately accept those of the other people on their team. As we mentioned earlier, a key concept the workplace is beginning to accept is that personality is just as much a component of workplace diversity as age, gender, race, and ethnic origin.

What the technicians' team finally realized was that the other team members' stated positions and ways of thinking were simply different from theirs instead of "wrong." This newfound tolerance for an alternative position made it possible for them to begin to collaborate, including points that were important to both the O−− members and the O= and O+ members. As Bruce Tuckman (1965) would say, the team moved from their stuck position in the storming stage of team development through the norming stage and on to the performing stage. After we facilitated the first few meetings, we set up team roles: facilitator, recorder, spokesperson, timekeeper, and member. The team defined each of the roles and selected people for the roles based on their Big Five profiles. Through conversations with management and with the chemists and engineers, the team members began to realize their own ability to obtain the resources they needed. When they completed their original assignment within four months and began to turn their attention toward other problems, management rewarded all of them with jackets bearing the company logo, which they wore with a great deal of pride. The team even gave the consultant one!

Realistically, not all teams have fairy-tale outcomes in the workplace. Some teams are in constant conflict and have to be abandoned or completely re-formed. However, using the Big Five with teams, especially in their early stage of development (which Tuckman calls the forming stage), can clearly help to explain individual differences and highlight each person's strengths before these differences can erupt into conflict that adversely affects communication. When the team encounters the storming stage, as it eventually will, it's very helpful to have the Big Five knowledge already in place and in use to give the team a language with which to talk about the differences and resolve the conflicts.

An important learning from this and all of the case studies throughout this book is that Big Five personality profiling is just the starting point. The Big Five model can help us by pointing out likely difficulties in team dynamics, challenges we may experience during team meetings, or subtleties that could make our daily communication and interactions more pleasant or understandable as we engage in the day to day work of our team. The profiles help us to depersonalize our stronger and weaker tendencies, keeping us from calling them right or wrong. Our scores on the Big Five model simply become who we are. At that point, we shouldn't just stop with the knowledge of our personalities; we ultimately have to create strategies to deal with our personality tendencies so that the team can accomplish its work.

Simply holding a fun, half-day team-building session where team members share their scores without expecting the session to lead to any concrete discussions, conflicts, changes, or job reorganizations is truly an empty way to use any personality instrument. This is often the reason that some people have come to distrust the value of these instruments in the workplace. The real value of the Big Five model comes from applying it to our daily activities and deciding how it can help us to improve our workplace. The scores and Big Five results should then lead us forward to create plans, team action items, goals, and tactics that capitalize on the strengths of our personalities.

Teams may have problems because the people in them are too much alike, or they may falter because of internal politics concerning who is placed on the team. In the next chapter, we'll review the basics of selection, including ways to use the Five-Factor Model in identifying the best person for the job or the team.

13

Selection

66 *There is hardly a person living concerning some essential part of whose character there are not differences of opinion even among his intimate acquaintances; and a single action, or conduct continued only for a short time, goes a very little way toward ascertaining it.* **99**

—*John Stuart Mill*

Reducing Risk in Hiring Decisions

ordon Allport relished lamenting that the individual person was on the one hand unknowable, and on the other rock solid, saying, "All the general laws of human behavior taken together cannot possibly tell the psychologist what his best friend will do come Christmas" (1937, p. 559). Further complicating the already difficult task of knowing a person well enough to predict future behavior is the fact that the single individual has multiple selves, and these selves are perceived differently by people with different points of view. I (Pierce) am a musician, a researcher, a writer, a speaker, a parent, a husband, a teacher, and a basketball fan, and each of my roles is perceived differently by family, friends, customers, vendors, co-workers, ministers, artists, scientists, politicians, social workers, poets, and baby-sitters. Yet in spite of this maelstrom of roles and perceptions, I carry the same set of genes with me everywhere I go. Allport (1937, p. 559) says, "All this biosocial variability [is] like reflecting mirrors in an amusement park. Each distorts the face and figure in a different way—lengthening, shortening, expanding, and contracting it—while still keeping some sort of likeness. But all the while there is only *one* person present; he remains single however much the reflecting images may multiply."

This chapter is about selecting future workers. With such diversity of perception, how could one dare decide with confidence who should get a job? Twentieth-century English sportsman George John Whyte-Melville rejected this dilemma outright when he stated, "In the choice of a horse and a wife, a man must please himself, ignoring the opinion and advice of friends." We're reminded of a client who needed to hire three employees, each of whom would perform a role for which our client had no previous hiring experience. We gave the hiring manager three forms to complete, one for each job. The three jobs were dramatically different: team facilitator, statistical analyst, and marketing assistant. Our three forms were designed to help the hiring manager identify the ideal scores for these specific jobs on each of the facets of the Big Five. When he returned the forms to us, two features were remarkable. First, all three forms were identical. He had failed to discriminate between the three roles, asking for the same facets for each job. Second, each facet score he asked for was identical to his own personal scores on the Big Five. He was asking for clones of himself! When we pointed this out to him, he was appropriately amused. We filled out new forms together, eschewing the narcissistic tendency into which we so easily fall. Like Whyte-Melville, our client was trying to please himself by hiring people like himself, rather than building a team with a diversity of talents and resources. He knew better, but the instinct to hire clones of ourselves is indeed strong.

> *"Can't act. Can't sing. Balding. Can dance a little."*
> —MGM executive about Fred Astaire's screen test

Establishing a Basis for Selection

In making the selection decision, the following assumptions are helpful:

1. Given this multiplicity of roles and relationships, the best estimate of the core self or trait infrastructure (or the "rock

bottom," as Charley, in *Death of a Salesman,* would say) is one's own self-image. This is best assessed by a valid and reliable test completed by the individual under consideration.

2. Additional information on individuals under consideration can be obtained by having raters complete questionnaires about them. This can be expensive and time-consuming, yet in high-risk hiring decisions, it can be well worth the expense. Obtaining only one or two raters' opinions frequently just adds more mirrors to the original image; however, five or more raters' opinions can provide some degree of corroboration of the individual's self-image. But whom do you ask to serve as a rater: spouse, former boss, former spouse, partner, co-worker, customer, vendor, child, teacher? Each will have a different perspective, and the individual will have shown a different face to each of them.

3. It's best to use a diverse sample of raters, rather than either (a) one or two raters or (b) a half-dozen raters who have the same relation to the individual. These two cases become a matter of "He says, she says," whereas with diverse raters it becomes possible to triangulate the rock bottom.

4. No single test, inventory, questionnaire, or reference is sufficient to make the hiring decision; a variety of selection protocols should be used.

We have prepared a composite listing of the validity coefficients associated with the many different kinds of selection protocols used in industry. This composite, which is presented in Table 13.1, is based on the studies contained in a half-dozen standard industrial psychology textbooks. Notice that the highest predictive validity coefficient is .53, for mental and psychomotor tests. If any single selection test were able to predict future performance perfectly, its validity coefficient would be 1.00. Does the failure of any one test to significantly crack the .50 predictive coefficient barrier mean that selection testing is a hopeless endeavor? No. Just as an individual has many roles, she or he also has many sets of attributes—traits, talents, skills, credit history, and so forth—and can be assessed in a variety of ways, including self-report tests, reference checks, assessment centers, interviews by panels and individuals, and professional psychological assessments. By pooling a variety of these tests, each of which relates to the demands of the job in question, we can approach a *combined* predictive validity of 1.00. In statistical terms, this is known as a "multiple R," or multiple prediction coefficient.

Each test that's used must be validated. Choosing a test just because it seems good opens companies to the possibility of a legal challenge. The courts are full of examples of employers who used tests for selection without first attempting to validate them. In the next section of this chapter, we'll discuss the ingredients of a proper validity study whose goal is to determine the degree to which a particular test—from a paper-and-pencil personality inventory to a credit check—is relevant to the ability to perform in a particular job.

Establishing the Validity of a Selection Test

Validity comes in two forms: (1) when incumbent high performers are currently in the job and available for assessment and (2) when no assessable incumbents exist, either because the incumbents can't be assessed or because there are none (as when a job is new to the organization). First, let's take a look at the process for conducting a validity study when assessable incumbents exist. This process has seven steps:

1. *Agree on the performance criteria:* Agreeing on applicable performance criteria can be tricky. A panoply of such criteria populate the workplace, including but not limited to sales volume, sales margin, overall performance, specific aspects of performance, rate of salary increases, tenure, learning curve, grades, and class standing.

2. *Determine the learning curve:* How long does it take for a new employee to demonstrate performance in a way that allows management to confidently assess whether hiring the employee was a good or bad decision? Assembly workers may require only two to three weeks to reach peak performance, whereas sales representatives could take five to seven months, R&D chemists eighteen to twenty-four months. Eliminate incumbents from the initial validity study who have not yet completed the learning curve; if you wish, you can use them as part of a predictive study at some later time.

3. *Identify high and low performers:* Use existing data, such as performance appraisals or sales records, if they are valid

Validity Coefficients for Commonly Used Selection Tests.	**TABLE 13.1**

Selection Test or Procedure	Average Predictive Validity
Mental and psychomotor tests	.53
Job knowledge tests	.50
Skill tests	.44
Big Five test with job analysis	.40
Biographical information forms	.35
Structured interviews	.34
Assessment centers	.25
Personality tests (pre–Big Five)	.24
Class rank	.21
Exporienoo	.10
Traditional interviews	.17
Reference checks	.13
College grades	.13
Vocational interest tests	.10
Amount of education	.10
Handwriting analysis	.00
Projective personality tests	.00
Age	.00

and reliable. Develop new measurement tools for performance appraisal, if needed. Test all incumbents or only the high and low performers, depending on the situation. Use clusters, not arbitrary cutoffs, and don't use only the top and bottom 20 percent when a clear cluster reveals a break at different points.

4. *Administer the predictive instrument, such as a Big Five test:* Plan whether 100 percent of the job group or just the high and low performers will take the test.

5. *Determine the factors and facets that relate to high and low performance:* Examine the scatter pattern. One of three relationships can exist between the predictor variable and the performance variable: *linear,* either positive (the higher one is, the higher the other is) or negative (the higher one is, the lower the other is); *curvilinear* (extreme scores on the

predictor variable are associated with low scores on performance, while moderate scores on the predictor variable are associated with high scores on performance); or *nonexistent* (no relationship is found between the predictor and performance).

6. *Integrate your findings into the selection procedure:* For small-sample studies, you might use a rough template to eyeball the fit between candidates and your new ideal profile. For larger samples, you could compute a simple correlation coefficient between predictor and performance score, or you could find a multiple R, using the Big Five along with other tests. Establish the relative weights for all tests and subtests and determine each individual's weighted score.

7. *Collect ongoing data and reanalyze the data in several years:* What we have described up to this point is a concurrent validity study; however, the courts look much more favorably on predictive validity studies. In order to determine the ability of a test to actually predict future performance, you must collect performance data on the tested individuals after they have been hired and have passed their learning curves. (If some of these terms pique your curiosity, take a look at Robert Rose's 1993 book, *Practical Issues in Employment Testing,* which provides a readable introduction to the basic concepts and terms associated with employment testing.)

> **"The only problem I really have in the outfield is with fly balls."**
> —Carmelo Martinez,
> San Diego Padres outfielder

Hiring Case Study 1

A Validity Study with Incumbents

A company that sold and serviced farm equipment wanted help in improving its selection process for managers and supervisors. The company had 100 management staff and used a sophisticated performance appraisal system that passed the test of validity and reliability. Twenty-three of the managers clustered at the top two rungs of the scale (6 and 7 on a seven-point scale), while nineteen clustered at the bottom three rungs

(1, 2, and 3 on a seven-point scale). It was clearly desirable to try to clone the members of the high group and avoid the members of the low one in future hiring and promotion decisions. We administered the Big Five inventory to all 100 managers; Figure 13.1 shows how they fared as a total group.

Notice the unusually high A score for this group of managers. Recall from the discussion in Chapter Eight that the ideal management profile includes a 45 on A, which is a somewhat tougher score than the 53 registered by these service managers. This reflects their highly developed corpo-

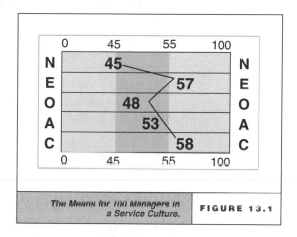

The Means for 100 Managers in a Service Culture.   **FIGURE 13.1**

rate culture, which emphasizes excellent service and the philosophy that the customer is always right. This corporate philosophy encourages trust, openness, helpfulness, and agreeableness. Not your typical management team. Before looking at the results of the validity study, try your hand at predicting how the high-performing group of twenty-three managers would compare to these group means, recalling our discussion of the ideal manager from Chapter Eight. They clearly diverged on each of the five factors, with mean differences of anywhere from two to ten standard score points.

The comparison of high- and low-performing managers' mean scores appears in Figure 13.2. How close were your pre-

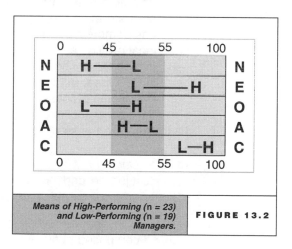

Means of High-Performing (n = 23) and Low-Performing (n = 19) Managers.   **FIGURE 13.2**

dictions? All of the results were in accord with the ideal manager leader profile detailed in Chapter Eight. The higher-performing managers were less reactive (N–), more outgoing (E+), somewhat more visionary (O+), a bit tougher (A–), and just slightly more ambitious and disciplined (C+). Most of these managers were probably promoted originally on the basis of their C+ profile. People who are organized, ambitious, deliberate, and focused tend to be promoted, unless they somehow manage to shoot themselves in the foot. The most dramatic difference between the two groups was in Extraversion, where the high performers scored almost one whole standard deviation (ten points) higher than the lower performers. This suggests that effectiveness in communication plays a large part in determining the performance level of managers.

Hiring Case Study 2
A Validity Study with No Assessable High Performers

Recently an organization with some ten thousand employees asked us to assist them in selecting an internal audit manager. The position was new, its role having been handled before as part of another manager's job. Because we could not determine the Big Five profile for this position by assessing one or more high-performing incumbents, we set out to identify an ideal profile based on the selection committee's understanding of the job description they had designed. Remember that determining the ideal Big Five profile for the position was only one part of the overall process, and that sound selection processes involve the use of multiple tests, each of which is validated separately. Here are the steps we used:

1. *Come up with a comprehensive job description:* Either obtain a job description from an outside source, develop your own, or use a combination of the two methods.

2. *Convene the selection committee:* Our committee was composed of five future peers of this internal audit manager, two superiors, and three human resource specialists.

3. *Review the job description with the committee:* Read it silently, then discuss it and ensure agreement on key issues. The facilitator should ask provocative questions and point out

trade-off areas, for example, "You're asking for both sociability and solitariness. Does that mean you want a balance, or is one more important than the other?"

4. *Have each member of the committee individually complete the Job Profiler©:* The Job Profiler is a worksheet, available from *Cent*ACS, that contains verbal anchors, from very low to very high, for each of the five levels of the Big Five facets.

5. *Have the committee negotiate an ideal profile:* Committee members should agree on the anchors for each facet that would be acceptable in an ideal internal audit manager.

6. *Develop a template:* Based on the ideal profile identified in step 5, create a template that will highlight how each finalist compares to the ideal.

7. *Administer the Big Five inventory to the finalists:* In this case, we used the NEO PI-R. Now that it's available, we could use the WorkPlace Big Five ProFile.

8. *Compare the finalists' Big Five profiles to the ideal template.*

9. *Validate the ideal template after performance data become available:* After the new internal audit manager has had a few years on the job, revisit the ideal template in light of her or his performance.

The outcome of this process was a template. A copy of the actual template is included here as Figure 13.3. The four areas of the template with double borders were "knockout" facets: if a candidate didn't score in that range of a facet, he or she was automatically eliminated from further consideration. Notice also that aesthetics (O2) is blacked out. This reflects the selection committee's judgment that this facet wasn't relevant to the job at all and that any score would be acceptable.

Some decision makers want more than facet and factor scores; they want you to predict how an individual is likely to perform on specific job competencies. It is for this reason that we developed the list of fifty-four competencies we will present in Table 15.1, along with their associated Big Five trait infrastructures. By obtaining an individual's Big Five scores, we can estimate his or her probable per-

NEO PI-R JOB PROFILE

DATE: March 24, 1998

JOB: Internal Audit Manager

Distribution: 7% 24% 38% 24% 7%

Facet	Low pole						High pole
N1: Worry	Relaxed; calm; unconcerned						Worrying; uneasy
N2: Anger	Composed; slow to anger						Quick to feel anger
N3: Discouragement	Rarely discouraged; guilt-free						Easily discouraged
N4: Self-consciousness	Hard to embarrass; status-free						More easily embarrassed
N5: Impulsiveness	Resists urges easily; not excitable						Easily tempted; excitable
N6: Vulnerability	Handles stress and crises well						Difficulty coping; vulnerable
E1: Warmth	Reserved; formal						Affectionate; friendly; intimate
E2: Gregariousness	Seldom seeks company						Gregarious; prefers company
E3: Assertiveness	Stays in background						Assertive; speaks up; leads
E4: Activity	Leisurely pace						Vigorous pace
E5: Excitement seeking	Low need for thrills						Craves excitement
E6: Positive emotions	Less exuberant						Cheerful; optimistic

FIGURE 13.3 Template for Internal Audit Manager.

Facet	Low	High
O1: Fantasy	Focuses on here and now	Imaginative; daydreams
O2: Aesthetics	Uninterested in art	Appreciates art and beauty
O3: Feelings	Ignores or discounts feelings	Values all emotions
O4: Actions	Prefers the familiar	Prefers variety; tries new things
O5: Ideas	Narrower intellectual focus	Broad intellectual curiosity
O6: Values	Dogmatic; conservative	Open to reexamining values
A1: Trust	Cynical; skeptical	Thinks others honest, well-intentioned
A2: Straightforwardness	Guarded; stretches truth	Straightforward, frank
A3: Altruism	Reluctant to get involved	Willing to help others
A4: Compliance	Aggressive; competitive	Yields under conflict; defers
A5: Modesty	Feels superior to others	Self-effacing; humble
A6: Tender-mindedness	Hardheaded; insensitive	Tender-minded; easily moved
C1: Competence	Often feels unprepared	Feels capable and effective
C2: Order	Unorganized; unmethodical	Well-organized; neat; tidy
C3: Dutifulness	Casual about obligations	Guided by conscience; reliable
C4: Achievement striving	Low need for achievement	Driven to achieve success
C5: Self-discipline	Procrastinates; distracted	Focused on completing tasks
C6: Deliberation	Spontaneous; makes hasty decisions	Thinks carefully before acting

Source: Adapted with permission from P. T. Costa, Jr., and R. R. McCrae, NEO PI-R: Professional Manual, Odessa, FL: Psychological Assessment Resources, 1992, and personal correspondence. NEO PI-R: Professional Manual copyright by P. T. Costa, Jr., R. R. McCrae, and the Psychological Assessment Resources, 1992.

formance level on each of these fifty-four competencies. We call this resulting profile the *Cent*ACS Professional Competency Profile. A sample, complete with a narrative profile, is available by contacting us at *Cent*ACS. The report is a bit long for inclusion in this book!

Part
Three

The

Wisdom

of

Developing

People

Solomon as Manager

14

Nature Versus Nurture

What You Can Change, and What You Can't

From the beginning of language, humans have coined expressions to keep things straight. From "Me Tarzan, you Jane" through the redbirds and bluebirds of elementary school, words have helped us to classify, coordinate, command, and understand. In the realm of personality, Plato wrote of "gold" dispositions from which leaders were supposedly forged, "silver" for their "auxiliaries," and "bronze" dispositions that yielded craftsmen (*The Republic,* Book III). Empedocles (c. 450 B.C.) claimed that some dispositions were like air (warm and moist), some like fire (warm and dry), others like earth (cool and dry) or water (cool and moist). Somewhat more recently, Tennessee Ernie Ford crooned, "Some people say a man is made out of mud," while others have said that boys are made of "snakes and snails, and puppy dogs' tails"; girls of "sugar and spice, and everything nice."

With the exception of Tarzan's feeble greeting, all these other quotes are attempts to speak the language of personality traits. The Romans created masks for actors to wear on stage. Some masks wore smiles, others smirks, still others grimaces. The masks provided clues to early audiences about the fairly consistent pattern of behavior they could expect from the actors wearing them. This type of mask bore the name *persona,* providing the basis of our modern word *personality.* Personality, then, is the pattern of behavior by which we are recognized. Our unique patterns of behavior become our signature. In fact, people with distinctive traits frequently have given their names to these traits: Byronic, Calvinistic, chauvinistic, Ciceronian, Christlike, Dionysian, Falstaffian, Faustian, lesbian, Machiavellian, and narcissistic, among others.

Ever since the Greeks saw personality as a blend of the four elements, the Western world has habitually used four dimensions to describe individual differences. Not always earth, air, fire, and water, but typically four dimensions. Shakespeare called them phlegmatic, choleric, sanguine, and melancholic. Native Americans saw the four points of the compass associated with four animals and their associated qualities: eagle/east, squirrel/south, bear/west, and buffalo/north. More recently, some human resource developers have categorized us as blues, yellows, reds, and greens, while others have labeled us doves, ostriches, pheasants, and eagles (feel like a d-o-p-e?).

The Game Behind the Name

Trait names describe the structure of personality and are the historic beginning point for understanding and discussing it. Just as we can't play cards without names for the Jack, Queen, King, Ace, and so forth, we can't discuss personality without names for its parts, and by the end of this book, you'll have names for personality parts "in spades."

But what is the game behind the name? If gregariousness names a trait, how do we explain the trait itself? A personality trait has two components: the raw material with which we're born and the finished product toward which we evolve. Our fixed skeleton and the way we add fat or muscle to it. Our inborn nature and how our environment nurtures it. Shakespeare knew this dual source of dispositional characteristics when, in *The Tempest* (Act IV, scene i, lines 188–190), he had Prospero describe the incorrigible Caliban:

A devil, a born devil, on whose nature
Nurture can never stick; on whom my pains,
Humanely taken, are all lost, quite lost . . .

Here Shakespeare concluded that Caliban's inherited nature was so extreme that no environment, education, training, or coaching could soften it. Charles Darwin essentially agreed with Shakespeare, finding that we are born with natures that have proved to have some kind of survival value. Darwin didn't know how the human genome worked, but he had confidence that something like what we know today as DNA was working its magic. Or rather, its science.

In the twentieth century, the argument between nature and nurture came to a head. The new Darwinians preached nature, and the behaviorists preached nurture. In 1925, behaviorist John Watson said, "Give me a dozen healthy infants, well-formed, and my own specified world to bring them up in and I'll guarantee to take any one at random and train him to become any type of specialist I might select—doctor, lawyer, artist, merchant-chief and, yes, even beggar-man and thief, regardless of his talents, penchants, tendencies, abilities, vocations, and race of his ancestors" (p. 82). In the same year, Margaret Mead set sail for Samoa and, in her effort to please her mentor, Franz Boas, eventually published *Coming of Age in Samoa* (1928), a work that is widely regarded today as bad science, full of excessive zeal to prove the dominance of social and cultural determinism over Darwinism.

In support of Watson and Mead, Walter Mischel, in *Personality and Assessment* (1968), claimed that nature did not exist, that all behavior was learned and situational, and that how we behave depends totally on the cumulative effects of experience. The debate even reared its head on the popular stage, as evidenced from W. S. Gilbert's line from Act II of *Princess Ida:*

Darwinian man, though well-behaved,
At best is only a monkey shaved.

Roaring right back, E. O. Wilson, in his influential work *Sociobiology* (1975), established an irreversible foothold for the Darwinians in the study of human behavior.

Nevertheless, neither side won. Instead, both sides did. Today, personality theorists conclude that traits have both inherited and learned components. The inherited part is usually referred to as *temperament,* and the learned part is usually called *personality.* Personality, then, is the result of what we're born with after it's been mingled with what the world has brought our way. Or, as Robert Ornstein (1993, p. 24) phrases it, "Individuals need the world to give them their individuality, yet the world can only develop what we've inherited."

A personality trait name is a convenient way to refer to a collection of inherited and learned behaviors that tend to occur together in the same person. For example, we've talked about gregariousness. Here are some examples of possible inherited and learned ingredients of that highly sociable trait:

Inherited Elements of Gregariousness

- The set point of our motoric nervous system

- Everyday levels of the monoamine oxydase enzyme, which are lower in more gregarious people

- Membership in the AB blood group

- Activity level (the number of foot, leg, arm, head, and hand movements per minute from the time we're swimming in the womb)

Learned Elements of Gregariousness

- The level of noise in the womb and early home environment (for example, blaring radios or television sets, or public transportation roaring by outside the window)

- Encouragement for reading, writing, and keyboarding versus public speaking and conversing

- Racial, ethnic, religious, or other cultural influences

- The pervasive influence of the current dominant peer group

In these lists, genes determine the levels of the inherited elements and environment determines the levels of the learned elements. Our inborn, fixed temperament—the raw material of who we are—is based on the first list. The basic task of adding personality to temperament consists of swimming either with or against the currents dictated by our inheritance. As we've seen throughout this book, individual development is optimal when personal goals are compatible with how one is put together genetically. A person who is "nature-ally" gregarious may be a politician or a monk, but if a monk, then better a leader of monks—an abbot, say—than an anchorite praying continually in solitude.

Out of the debate of Darwin and Mead, of Wilson and Watson, voices called for common ground. The next two chapters summarize what has come of this debate, and how these voices have shaped a new approach to developing people in the workplace for the twenty-first century.

15

The Right Stuff

The Raw Material for Performance Competencies

As we asserted at the beginning of Chapter One, the primary value of studying personality in the workplace rests on the degree to which it will result in improved performance. Organizational performance, team performance, individual performance; performance based upon choosing the right people to begin with, as well as performance based upon coaching those who need to improve.

For decades we've witnessed hucksters of motivation, ex-quarterbacks turned cheerleaders—you know the drill. Such sources of motivation result in short-lived action, if any. Like psychotropic drugs, frequent doses are required in order to maintain the high. But what is motivation? The root of *motivation* contains the idea of being "in motion." One who is motivated is, by definition, moving, in action. Not a couch potato. Up and at 'em. To be motivated is to be

> **Eighty percent of success is showing up.**
>
> —*Woody Allen*

a part of the action, not a passive observer. Extraverts stay naturally in a gregarious mode, and Introverts stay naturally in a solitary mode. Therefore, according to our definition, Extraverts are motivated when they're being gregarious and Introverts are motivated when they're being solitary. At times we need cheerleaders around to spur us into action. Extraverts may need cheerleaders to exhort them into solitude, and Introverts may need cheerleaders to push them into gregariousness. But in this chapter, we'll see that the highest form of motivation, of being in action, occurs when we are pursuing a life that's consistent with the way we're put together. When we attempt to be something we're not, that's demotivating.

Motivation and Competency

In the workplace, motivation applies to individuals who are responsible for specific competencies. A competency is something in which you *compete*. When two people come together for a task, the more competent person will excel at the task. *Competence* (mastery of a competency), which has the same root as the word *compete,* is seen today as the essence of the "competitive" edge in the workplace.

When people are performing a competency at an acceptable level, all is well, and we would describe them as motivated. It's likely that much of the time when they're working at the competency, they're experiencing "flow," which Csikszentmihalyi (1990) describes as that satisfying state of involvement when we lose track of place and time. When people are not performing at an acceptable level, coaching is needed. Coaching is the process of analyzing an individual's performance with the goal of finding ways to improve it. Several classic books exist on the subject of coaching, or performance analysis, including those by Buckingham and Coffman (1999), Fournies (1999), Mager and Pipe (1997), Hersey and Blanchard (1988), and Robinson and Robinson (1995). Among these coaching models, one of the steps in analyzing a performance problem is to determine whether or not the performer's personality possesses the appropriate infrastructure for the underperformed competency.

This begs the question: what do we mean when we say that a personality profile does or does not fit a competency? Basically, one's personality can relate to a given competency in one of three ways:

1. *A trait equals a competency:* A personality trait can actually be the same thing as the competency itself. For example, the competency "organization" is the same thing as WorkPlace facet C2, organization. Measuring one measures the other, directly, one-to-one. (See Chapters Two–Six to review the facets.)

2. *Several traits equal a competency:* A combination of personality traits can actually be the same thing as the competency itself. For example, the competency "self-control" is the same thing as the combination of factors N– (Resilient), E– (Introvert), O– (Preserver), A+ (Adapter), and C+ (Focused).

3. *Traits are necessary, but not sufficient, to produce a competency:* A trait or a combination of traits can provide a basis, or natural springboard, for the competency, while not being the competency itself. For example, low scores on Extraversion, particularly facet E2, sociability, provide an excellent basis for becoming a good writer, but writing skills are different from Introversion and are not guaranteed by the fact of being introverted. Strong Extraverts, however, must learn to be comfortable being quiet and alone in order to develop writing skills.

Each of these three types of association between traits and competencies could be described as the trait *infrastructure* for a competency. In the first two cases, the trait infrastructure and the competency structure are identical. In the third case, the trait infrastructure is distinct from the competency structure but supportive of it.

Every competency talked about in today's workplace has an associated trait infrastructure. In Table 15.1 on pages 200–208, we list the fifty-four competencies we have found to be the most commonly discussed in the workplace. For each competency, we list its research basis, several identifiers, and the infrastructure associated with the competency; finally we indicate whether the trait infrastructure is type 1, 2, or 3. If you don't see your favorite competency, check the identifiers; it might be included under another wording. The facets in the table refer to the NEO PI-R; WorkPlace Big Five ProFile facet associations are available upon request from *Cent*ACS.

We should take a moment to explain how to read the infrastructure columns in Table 15.1. These five columns contain abbreviated factor and facet names along with the direction of the relationship. Within each column, you may find some combination of letters and numbers. A letter with a plus sign indicates that higher scores on the factor identified in that column are associated with the competency for that row, a letter with a minus sign suggests that lower scores on that factor are associated with the competency, and a letter with an equal sign indicates that the competency is associated with midrange scores on that factor.

You will see, for example, N– in the "Negative Emotionality" column and the "Responsibility acceptance" row. This means that it's more natural for people who are low in N to accept responsibility than it is for those with higher scores in N. If no letter appears, but only numbers, the factor as a whole isn't associated with the competency; however, individual facets (or subfactors) of that factor are. Within a column, you'll notice that we've stacked letters and numbers to indicate groupings of similar relationships. So in the "Responsibility acceptance" row, you see 1– just under N–, and 6–– on the bottom of the "stack." This means that lower scores on facet N1 are *moderately* associated with accepting responsibility, and lower scores on facet N6 are *strongly* associated with the same competency. If two or more numbers are grouped together, the scores on all of the facets are associated with the competency; for example, A245– in the "Ambition" row indicates that lower scores on all three of the facets A2, A4, and A5 are associated with ambition. In this case, the main factor, agreeableness, is not associated with the competency, but the letter appears with the numbers for clarity. The letter must appear by itself on the first row of a stack in order to indicate that the main factor is associated with the competency. Note that for "Ambition," C has three plus signs, indicating that higher scores on C have an extremely strong association with ambition. In other words, the number of signs suggests the strength of the association.

The Effect of Trait Excess and Deficiency on Competencies

Although it's beyond the scope of this book, it's interesting to note that each of the fifty-four competency infrastructures in Table 15.1 can be weakened by having too much or too little of a single trait that forms a part of the whole infrastructure. We will look now at how one competency infrastructure is affected by variations in the individual traits within the infrastructure. We encourage you to engage in a similar exercise with competencies that are of particular interest to you.

The competency whose infrastructure we have chosen to analyze is "listening." Two reasons shaped this choice: first, it employs four out of the five traits, and second, it has a universally high value, regardless of industry or job. Our study of the research leads us to identify the following Big Five infrastructure as the ideal platform for the listening competency: N–E–A+C+.

> *"One of the best ways to persuade others is with your ears . . . by listening to them."*
> —Dean Rusk

How might our overall performance as a listener be affected by excesses or deficiencies in each of these four traits?

Too much N: Excessive reaction to a speaker can dampen the speaker's desire to disclose fully. Often individuals, especially those who are themselves reactive (N+) and who tend to defer to others (A+), feel the need to exert more control in their speech when talking with highly reactive people.

Too little N: Not enough reaction (that is, excessive calmness) can be interpreted as an unfeeling, uncaring, or preoccupied attitude.

Too much E: Clearly, people who talk too much listen too little! Recall the comment made by Tony Hillerman's Navajo detective Joe Leapfoot in *Coyote Waits*. Leapfoot's sidekick says that there's no need to interview a witness because they see an FBI agent leaving the witness's dwelling. The wise Navajo detective observes: "Ah, but we will get the information that the white man was too impatient to hear!" Navajo culture places such a high value on listening that rituals have been developed to discourage interruptions: for example, in a ceremony, only the person holding the ceremonial pipe (also known as the "talking stick") is allowed to speak.

Too little E: People with dramatically low E may find it difficult to listen for an extended period, because too much stimulation drains them of energy.

TABLE 15.1 The CentACS Professional Competency Profile: The Fifty-Four Most Common Competencies, with Their Identifiers, Associated Big Five Trait Infrastructure, Type of Infrastructure, and Research References.

Competency	Research References	Identifiers	Big Five Trait Infrastructure					Type
			Negative Emotionality	Extraversion	Openness	Agreeableness	Conscientiousness	
Action orientation	Ben-Zur and Wardi (1994); Morr and Howard (1999)	Displays a sense of urgency Is a speedy and timely decision maker Is ambitious and driven	N+	E++ 3+ 4++	O−	A− 14−	C− 4++ 6−−	2
Adherence to policy	Horner (1996); Kyl-Heku and Buss (1996); Cialdini, Trost, and Newsom (1995); Yik and Tang (1996)	Adheres to industry guidelines Is prone to follow established procedures Tends to go by the book	N+	E−	O−	A+	C+	2
Ambiguity and paradox, comfort with	Howard (2000a)	Can act even though the details are unresolved Is comfortable leaving issues open and waiting for resolution or answers Is at ease with theory and the unknown	N− 1236−	E+ 234+	O++ 1346+ 5++			2
Ambition	Furnham, Crump, and Whelan (1997); Costa and McCrae (1992)	Has a strong sense of career Has a sense of vision and purpose Wants to have impact and influence; is committed to making a difference	N− 36−	E+ 34+	O+ 3+	A245−	C+++	2
Analytical thinking	Furnham, Crump, and Whelan (1997)	Needs to understand and have insight Is good at and enjoys solving problems Is comfortable with and good at formulating strategy			O+ 15+			1
Business acumen	Furnham, Crump, and Whelan (1997)	Maximizes revenue, net income, and cash flow Is comfortable containing costs and making collections Uses resources wisely and to advantage	N−	E+	O−	A−	C+ 16+	3

Competency	References	Behaviors						Type
Change, comfort with	Furnham, Crump, and Whelan (1997); McDaniel (1992); Costa and McCrae (1992)	Welcomes improvements on a small or large scale Seeks a better way Lives and breathes continual improvement	N– 4–	E+ 3+	C++ 5+	A=	C–	2
Competitiveness	Yik and Tang (1996); Cochran (1998)	Has the courage to take risks Cannot rest until the contest is over Is energized by competition and the need to win	N–	E+	O+	A– 45–	C+	2
Computer and keyboarding skills	Cialdini, Trost, and Newsom (1995); de Fruyt and Mervielde (1997); Hayes, Roehm, and Castellano (1994); Howard (2000a)	Can focus on the here and now Is patient paying close attention to detail Is careful to avoid errors	N+ 136– 4+++	E– 3–	O=	A+	C+ 5+	3
Creativity	Costa and McCrae (1992)	Personally adds value to any task Is innovative and resourceful; is inventive Can dream up new marketing and other business strategies		E+ 46+	O+ 12345+	A1+	C– 26–	2
Decision-making skills	Morr and Howard (1999)	Has a reputation for high-quality decisions Does not put off decisions inappropriately Seldom changes mind; makes decisions that stick	N– 2– 13456––	E+ 16+ 34++	O+ 56+	A–	C++ 123456++	2
Delegation	Morr and Howard (1999)	Is comfortable directing and controlling the work of others Has the patience to provide necessary information or other support when delegating Is courageous in confronting others when necessary	N– 1346–	E+ 1246+ 3+	O+ 156+	A–	C+ 123456+	2
Development of personnel	Kyl-Heku and Buss (1996); Howard (2000a)	Shares expertise with anyone interested Is sought after for coaching, training, orientation Helps others plan their careers	N–	E+ 123456+	C3+	A++ 13456+	C14+	3

Type: 1 = The trait equals the competency; 2 = Several traits equal the competency; 3 = The traits are necessary, but not sufficient, to produce a competency.

TABLE 15.1 Continued.

Competency	Research References	Identifiers	Big Five Trait Infrastructure					Type
			Negative Emotionality	Extraversion	Openness	Agreeableness	Conscientiousness	
Diplomacy	Furnham, Crump, and Whelan (1997); Saucier and Goldberg (1998)	Has the interpersonal savvy for maintaining relationships Is easy to work with Maintains good relations with a variety of people	N2–	E+ 126+	O+	A++		2
Diversity, comfort with	Gaines and Reed (1995)	Adapts appropriately to cultural differences Enjoys being around people of different religions, races, geography, values Has a reputation for fairness and ease of working with all kinds of people	N–		O+	A+		3
Entrepreneurship	Furnham, Crump, and Whelan (1997)	Continually seeks new products or markets Works well under pressure Is consumed by the desire to succeed in business; is willing to risk it all	N–	E+	O+	A–	C+	2
Facilitation	Howard and Howard (1993)	Is effective at managing conflict situations Is good at negotiating for win-win solutions Can keep personal ego out of the discussion; brings others out	N=	E=	O=	A=	C=	2
Flexibility	Furnham, Crump, and Whelan (1997)	Bends policy when appropriate Is comfortable wearing many hats Is willing to shift priorities as needed	N–	E+	O+	A+	C–	2
Follow-through	Howard (2000a)	Focus remains on priorities; perseveres; delivers Doesn't let the details fall between the cracks Stays with a project to its conclusion	N256–	E36–	O– 15——	A3+	C+ 1+ 46–++ 235+++	2

Competency	References	Description	N	E	O	A	C	Type
Future orientation/ visionary outlook	Howard (2000b)	Prefers thinking strategically to thinking tactically Naturally considers the downstream implications of present-day decisions Dreams about possibilities for future products, markets, and methods		E1346+	O++ 1345+ 2++	A36+	C+ 14+	2
Hiring and staffing	Howard and Howard (1993)	Has a reputation for good judgment about people Keeps politics and personal bias out of people decisions Makes selection decisions that result in good performers	N=	E=	O=	A=	C=	3
Humor	Forabosco and Ruch (1994); Howard (2000a, 2000b)	Can laugh at self from time to time Shows sensitivity toward others in exercising sense of humor Enjoys life; is spontaneous and playful	N4-	E++ 1+ 2345++ 6+++	O++ 1235+	A6+	C- 36-	2
Independently, comfort working	Johnson and Ostendorf (1993); Barrick and Mount (1993); Bigazzi, Kello, and Marciano (1999)	Is comfortable working alone when necessary Does not require close supervision Does not need others to provide structure	N-	E+	O++	A-	C+	2
Informing others	Howard (2000a)	Passes on information to co-workers Avoids power games involving holding certain information privately Takes pride in well-informed associates		E+ 2346+ 1++	O+ 35+	A13+	C13+	2
Integrity and trust	Johnson and Ostendorf (1993); Ones, Viswesvaran, and Schmidt (1995); Howard (2000a, 2000b)	Maintains confidentiality when requested Shows self-discipline in all areas Gains credibility through consistency and reliability	N- 356-			A+	C++ 1356+	2
Leadership	Furnham, Crump, and Whelan (1997); Johnson and Ostendorf (1993)	Takes responsibility for initiating necessary changes Enjoys taking the role of coordinator or director Can make the tough decisions when necessary	N- 36-	E++ 34+	O+ 3+	A- 245-	C++ 3+ 12456++	2

Type: 1 = The trait equals the competency; 2 = Several traits equal the competency; 3 = The traits are necessary, but not sufficient, to produce a competency.

TABLE 15.1 | Continued.

Competency	Research References	Identifiers	Big Five Trait Infrastructure					Type
			Negative Emotionality	Extraversion	Openness	Agreeableness	Conscientiousness	
Listening	Howard (2000a)	Can keep silent while others express themselves Keeps ego and personal needs out of the conversation Tries to understand others before expressing self	N36–	E16–		A+ 45+	C+ 356+	3
Managing through systems	Furnham, Crump, and Whelan (1997)	Understands how complex systems and processes interrelate Naturally and effectively monitors complex systems and intervenes as necessary Trusts the system to work, but revises it when needed	N–	E– 6+	O+ 15+			3
Meeting management	Morr and Howard (1999); Howard and Howard (1993)	Facilitates discussion effectively; encourages diverse inputs Uses time wisely; neither belabors points nor allows superficial treatment Develops an agenda and follows through	N=	E+ 126+	O=	A=	C=	3
Motivation of others	Howard (2000b)	Brings out the best in people Gives recognition to others in a fair and consistent manner Genuinely cares about other people	N– 346–	E++ 256+ 134++		A3+	C+ 15+ 4++	2
Numerical accuracy	Howard (2000a, 2000b)	Easily focuses on the task at hand Enjoys looking for patterns on pages of numbers Has a reputation for accurate numerical memory	N– 25–		O5+	A+ 34+	C+ 1345+	3
Objectivity	Howard (2000a, 2000b)	Evaluates impartially Keeps personal needs, values, and interests out of judgments Shows no reluctance to speak the truth	N–– 123456–	E5–		A+ 145+	C15+	2

Construct	References	Description	N	E	O	A	C	Type
Optimism	Cochran (1998); Furnham, Crump, and Whelan (1997)	Accepts failure as temporary and points to future success Accepts credit for successes Resists taking failure personally	N— 145— 36—	E++ 25+ 346++	O35+	A16+ 45—	C+ 13456+	2
Organization	Johnson and Ostendorf (1993)	Naturally keeps personal area neat Puts things away when finished for the day Assembles all necessary materials and information before starting a task					C++	1
Overseas work success, likelihood of	Azar (1995)	Accepts cultural differences Can subordinate personal discomfort to goal achievement Is curious; is attracted to the unknown	N—		O+		C+	3
Paperwork, comfort with	Anderson (1994); Costa and McCrae (1992)	Is comfortable with repetitious attention to detail Tends to avoid making errors and enjoys catching them Maintains accurate and timely records, files, and reports	N5—	E—	O—		C+ 5+	2
Performance focus	Piedmont and Weinstein (1994)	Avoids procrastination; pushes for results Manages time and priorities effectively Meets deadlines and other targets consistently		E+		A2—	C+ 12345+	2
Planning	Crant (1995); Howard (2000a, 2000b)	Has the habit of specifying steps for a project before implementing it Naturally thinks, talks, and writes about being prepared for the future Is proactive in anticipating future needs	N56—	E+ 4+		A5+	C++ 123456+	2
Political savvy	Howard and Howard (1993)	Is comfortable around people at all levels, both inside and outside the organization Stays aware of all needs and issues throughout the organization Can be appropriately tough or soft as necessary	N=	E=	O=	A=	C=	3

Type: 1 = The trait equals the competency; 2 = Several traits equal the competency; 3 = The traits are necessary, but not sufficient, to produce a competency.

TABLE 15.1 Continued.

Competency	Research References	Identifiers	Big Five Trait Infrastructure					Type
			Negative Emotionality	Extraversion	Openness	Agreeableness	Conscientiousness	
Presentation skills	Howard (2000a, 2000b)	Shows confidence when in front of groups; shows little or no evidence of self-consciousness or discomfort Enjoys being the spokesperson for the team and handling questions Takes pride in making an effective presentation with appropriate media	N146–	E+ 1346+	O+ 12356+	A6+	C1+	3
Quality orientation	Howard and Howard (1993)	Maintains high standards with staff and facility Effectively inspects and monitors for performance Shows a bias for proper maintenance, housekeeping, and adherence to requirements in general	N–		O=	A–	C+	3
Range of perspective and interests	Furnham, Crump, and Whelan (1997)	Seeks broad business knowledge, not just in one field Participates in activities outside the business (community, region, nation) Is active in professional or trade associations		E+ 12346+	O+ 5+			2
Responsibility acceptance	Horner (1996); Cochran (1998); Furnham, Crump, and Whelan (1997)	Handles complaints without passing the buck Has internal locus of control Stands alone when called for	N– 1– 6– –		O+	A–	C+	2
Risk taking	Saucier and Goldberg (1998); Johnson and Ostendorf (1993)	Is fearless in approaching the unknown Has an unquenchable curiosity Is spontaneous in pursuit of the unusual	N–	E++ 5+	O+	A–	C–	2
Safety orientation	Costa and McCrae (1992); Booth-Kewley and Vickers (1994); Avia and others (1995)	Tends to stay healthy Is cautious when operating equipment; respects good ergonomic design and principles Avoids impulsive behaviors	N–	E+ 5–	O–	A+	C+	2

Competency	References	Description	N	E	O	A	C	Type
Sales orientation	Howard (2000a, 2000b, n.d.)	Has pride in ability to persuade others Is optimistic; doesn't like to take no for an answer Mixes easily with others and genuinely wants to meet the needs of customers	N4–	E++ 123456++	O+ 1– 235+	A6+ 5–	C6–	3
Self-confidence	Johnson and Ostendorf (1993); Costa and McCrae (1992)	Typically feels that the situation is under control Is prepared; believes that self and processes will succeed Accepts all reasonable challenges	N343–	E++ 3+		A5–	C+ 1+	2
Self-control	Johnson and Ostendorf (1993)	Maintains composure in the face of temptation Is not known to be spontaneous or impulsive Tends to keep regular hours and follow regular patterns	N–	E–	O–	A+	C++	2
Self-development	Howard (2000a, 2000b)	Uses all available resources for personal improvement; seeks opportunities to learn Seeks and uses feedback; is open to criticism Nondefensively assesses own strengths and weaknesses	N– 346–	E+ 234+	O13–	A+ 1234+	C++ 236+ 145++	2
Service orientation	Howard (2000a, 2000b); Kyl-Heku and Buss (1996); King (1995)	Is driven by the desire to serve the customer; is focused on customer needs Responds as promptly as possible to customer needs and requests Knows customers, alliances, and partners well and supports them in appropriate ways	N+ 123456+	E+ 1+		A++ 1346+	C– 246–	3
Teamwork and cooperation	Morr and Howard (1999); Johnson and Ostendorf (1993); Wang (1997); Furnham, Crump, and Whelan (1997)	Is able to subordinate personal needs to team success Is willing to follow or lead based on the team's need; is approachable Is committed to building the spirit of the team; genuinely enjoys being a part of a team	N– 2–	E+ 126+	O+ 3+	A++ 3+	C+	2

Type: 1 = The trait equals the competency; 2 = Several traits equal the competency; 3 = The traits are necessary, but not sufficient, to produce a competency.

TABLE 15.1 Continued.

Competency	Research References	Identifiers	Big Five Trait Infrastructure						Type
			Negative Emotionality	Extraversion	Openness	Agreeableness	Conscientiousness		
Technical learning	Howard (2000a, 2000b)	Prefers mastering the details before moving on to the next level Shows mastery of knowledge about the job, whether about products, markets, or subject areas Eagerly seeks and assimilates new relevant technical information	N26–	E4+	O14–		C+ 123456+		3
Work-life balance	Brandstaetter (1994); Howard (2000a, 2000b)	Has a personal life beyond job and career Avoids the temptation to work excessively long hours Is neither a workaholic nor a freeloader	N=	E=	O=	A=	C=		3
Written communication	Howard (2000b)	Has the habit of taking the time and effort to put thoughts into writing Is concise and descriptive, keeping the reader in mind Keeps on top of regular written documentation	N+ 1346+	E46+	O+ 125+		C+ 145+		3

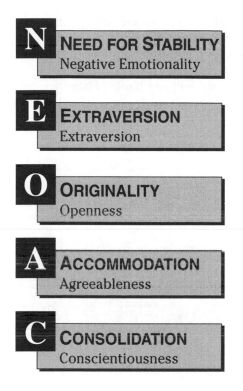

N NEED FOR STABILITY
Negative Emotionality

E EXTRAVERSION
Extraversion

O ORIGINALITY
Openness

A ACCOMMODATION
Agreeableness

C CONSOLIDATION
Conscientiousness

Too much A: People who are very high in A may agree too readily with the speaker, rather than questioning appropriately.

Too little A: People who are too low in A may, through pride, skepticism, or toughness, cause the speaker to feel inadequate or threatened in some way, thereby limiting the speaker's willingness to speak frankly and completely, especially if the A– is asking many questions. This is especially true when the speaker is N+ and/or A+ and the A– listener is also E+ and O+. People who are E+O+A– can be verbally overwhelming, limiting their value as listeners.

Too much C: People who are too high in C may be so focused on their goals that they ignore or don't hear comments that invite dialogue about subjects that aren't goal-related, but that are important to the speaker.

Too little C: People who are too low in C may be distracted from their listening role by competing stimuli in the environment, such as the telephone, music, other people talking, or unrelated tasks.

In the next chapter, we'll discuss what to do when an individual fails to perform an important competency at the desired level. We call these failures to perform "performance gaps," and they are often measured by what is referred to popularly as a 360° feedback instrument (see Leslie and Fleenor, 1998; Tornow, London, and CCL

Associates, 1998). Once an assessment device has identified such a performance gap, deciding on an appropriate strategy to remove the gap is paramount. Sometimes, however, we must choose not to remove the gap, but to work around it. Knowing when to reduce the gap and when to work around it is the subject of Chapter Sixteen.

16

When Pigs Can't Fly

Human Resource Optimization

> **You always think you're going to be the one that makes them act different.**
>
> —*Woody Allen,* Manhattan

Since John Watson's writings in the 1920s, we have more or less assumed that we could make anyone into anything if we just worked with the person long enough or hard enough. Year after year, trainers, developers, and performance analysts have built a multibillion-dollar business out of attempting to do this, as organizations dutifully have taken their employees and trained them in corporate universities. Yet we are told by Detterman and Sternberg (1993) and Baldwin and Ford (1988) that only about 10 percent of that training actually transfers to the workers' jobs. They estimate that 90 cents of every training dollar is wasted because most employees don't apply what they've been taught when they return to their jobs after training.

In terms of the nature-nurture debate we discussed in Chapter Fourteen, we have assumed that nurture rules and that we can tame any creature given the proper methods and technology. But we're finally beginning to learn that not all workers take equally well to all training. For some workers, new training sticks like Velcro, but for many others, it's deflected like water from Teflon. For human resource development professionals planning corporate training, for managers trying to develop new employees, for team members trying to help a co-worker learn a new procedure, the idea that you can't train everyone to do everything shakes the foundations of the existing training and development paradigm. This is the paradigm that, for example, looks at a performance gap (measured by the plethora of 360° tools currently available or the organization's newest employee performance review form) and automatically assumes that any gap between the employee's performance level and what we actually want from him or her can be closed by training or development in the specific performance area or competency.

> *"In my stars I am above thee; but be not afraid of greatness: some are born great, some achieve greatness, and some have greatness thrust upon them."*
>
> —Maria's note to Malvolio, in Shakespeare's *Twelfth Night*, Act II, scene 5

The radically new paradigm we propose is the Human Resource Optimizer Model (see the summary in Table 16.1). Anyone may become a Human Resource Optimizer (HRO). This new paradigm encourages us to look at a performance gap and ask a crucial question before deciding on the appropriate action: *Does the performer possess the appropriate raw material (ability and traits) to support development of the competency?* This paradigm assumes that every performance competency is associated with an ideal infrastructure that is composed of *talents* (or abilities) and Big Five *traits* (or behavioral dispositions). When a person fails to demonstrate a competency that we expect in a given job, or when a performance gap is identified that must be removed, the logical next question the HRO needs to ask is whether the solution is to

- Develop or compensate

- Train or offset

- Educate or work around

- Strengthen or redesign

- Provide practice or support

The New Paradigm for Human Resource Optimization.	**TABLE 16.1**

Old Paradigm	New Paradigm
Nurture is dominant	Nature is dominant
Weaknesses can be strengthened	Some weaknesses cannot be strengthened
Assess for gaps only	Assess for gaps *and* infrastructure
Train to improve	Develop or train if the infrastructure indicates *or*
	Support or coach if the infrastructure indicates *or*
	Compensate or redesign if the infrastructure indicates

Contemporary trainers often take trainees through the motions of a well-designed, interactive training program, wanting the program to change the trainees' lives but knowing that for many of them, the learning just will never stick, a decidedly bleak and expensive outcome for the organization. We recall talking to one such corporate trainer about an extremely introverted engineer who had just attended the trainer's three-day presentation skills workshop because his job required that he make presentations. Although the trainer had used every method and technique he had at his disposal including video feedback, glitzy graphics, visualization techniques, and the best materials, the E–– engineer's last presentation of the program was as painful as his first, both for him and for the other members of the class who listened to him. The engineer's basic trait infrastructure simply was not suited for making presentations. The trainer, meanwhile, was full of self-doubts about his ability to train others, questioning what he could or should have done differently to get through to the E–– engineer and "change" him.

Imagine sending a manager to a strategic planning workshop who has no ability to create mental images about the future (facet O1+). In order to identify the ideal infrastructure associated with this competency, the HRO professional will need a checklist of intelligence (talents and abilities) and traits such as the one shown in

Table 16.2. The traits are defined in terms of the WorkPlace Big Five ProFile, and intelligence is defined in terms of models by Robert Sternberg (1988), Howard Gardner (1983), and Elliott Jaques (1994). Recall that in Table 15.1, we presented the Big Five infrastructures for fifty-four competencies. The HRO model uses this type of personality trait infrastructure, in addition to using the other side of

TABLE 16.2	*Sample Infrastructure Checklist for the Competency "Strategic Planning," Using the Human Resource Optimizer Model.*	
Areas	*Elements*	*Requirements*
Traits **Big Five**	N E O A C	Not relevant Not relevant High, especially facet O1 Midrange Not relevant
Intelligence **Sternberg: Triarchic Model**	Meta (acquisition) Meta (planning) Meta (performance) Creative Judgment	High High Midrange High High
Gardner: Multiple Intelligences Model	Verbal Logical-mathematical Visual-spatial Auditory-musical Kinesthetic Interpersonal Intrapersonal Natural observation	High High Not relevant Not relevant Not relevant Midrange Not relevant High
Jaques: Model of Human Capability	Necessary experience and knowledge Necessary desire and drive Absence of self-defeating behaviors Time span ability	High High Midrange 25-year (Stratum VI)

Source: This checklist incorporates material from Robert J. Sternberg, *The Triarchic Mind: A New Theory of Human Intelligence,* New York: Viking Penguin, 1988; Howard Gardner, *Frames of Mind: The Theory of Multiple Intelligences,* New York: Basic Books, 1983; Elliott Jaques, *Human Capability,* Falls Church, VA: Cason Hall, 1994; and Pierce J. Howard, *The Owner's Manual for the Brain: Everyday Applications from Mind-Brain Research* (2nd ed.), Austin, TX: Bard Press, 2000c.

personality, or intelligence. The conventional paradigm for intelligence is undergoing a tremendous shift, with the old paradigm of verbal, numerical, and spatial reasoning giving way to a much more comprehensive one based on the work of Sternberg, Gardner, and Jaques. This paradigm shift has been described in some detail in Howard (2000c).

By using the infrastructure checklist, the HRO can identify the ideal mix of Big Five traits and other talents for yielding high performance in strategic planning. The HRO then can assess the individual using the checklist's models in order to determine if a gap exists, and if so, how large it is. Finally, the HRO will make a judgment: if the individual's infrastructure matches the ideal requirements for strategic planning, but a gap currently exists between his or her job performance on the strategic planning competency and what the organization expects, the HRO will use development (including, perhaps, training) to reduce the gap.

On the other hand, if the gap or "fit" between someone's infrastructure checklist and the ideal infrastructure for the competency contains large discrepancies, the HRO probably should not try to develop the individual but should look for some kind of compensation strategy or work-around solution instead. Only if a person possesses extraordinary personal motivation to reduce the gap should training be considered and, even then, it would be a high-risk decision in terms of either attaining the desired level of performance or facing potentially adverse consequences on his or her health.

Placing a person into a job that doesn't fit his or her nature is stressful and can result in long-term physical illnesses, ranging from asthma to heart disease and cancer. This can be especially taxing on people who score high on the Big Five N scale. The humane way to optimize a human resource who doesn't demonstrate the appropriate infrastructure for a particular competency, then, is to employ compensatory strategies such as these:

- Delegation of the competency to another worker
- Job redesign
- Reassignment or transfer to a more compatible team, department, or job culture
- Career change
- Industry change

The essential difference between developmental and compensatory strategies can be highlighted by two sets of action verbs:

Developmental	Compensatory
Teach	Offset
Learn	Substitute
Train	Work around
Educate	Redesign
Practice	Use a crutch
Study	Rely on others

If the fit between the ideal and actual infrastructures is not clear-cut, neither close nor remote, then an in-between strategy may be in order, such as supporting, mentoring, coaching, or adapting the job to the worker. Table 16.3 contrasts these three HRO strategies.

The following case studies may serve to illustrate the new HRO paradigm.

HRO Case Study 1

Sleepless in Charlotte

Jimmy was a National Basketball Association television producer who got so worked up during broadcast games in the evening that he couldn't get to sleep until four or five in the morning. He knew that this couldn't continue and consulted us for career counseling. After giving him a battery of tests and identifying the ideal infrastructure for his job, we spotted a significantly poor job fit. Jimmy had a very low threshold for stress, with an overall N+ score of 73. As a result, his tendency to worry and react was intensified by the low margin of error associated with live sports telecasts. As a temporary aid, we suggested that he engage in aerobic exercise to calm down after each stressful broadcast. This helped, but only marginally.

As Jimmy struggled with his sleeping difficulties and a continuing basketball season, he was asked to produce an ABC "Wide World of Sports" show. Because the show had a wider margin of error, it wasn't broadcast live in real time but was filmed first

The Three Strategies for Human Resource Optimization, Based on the Degree of Fit Between the Individual and Ideal Infrastructures.	TABLE 16.3

Competency Being Considered	*"Able to Initiate Effective Marketing and Advertising Techniques"*
Examples of competency when present	Doesn't wait to be told to take action. Ad strategies are fresh, not the same old ones.
Examples of competency when absent	May be creative and original, but doesn't appeal to the target market. May show initiative, but ads seem ordinary.

STRATEGY 1

Compensate (low rating + poor fit), using work-around tactics	Identify a creative resource, either on your team or outside, who can regularly feed you ideas that would appeal to your market profile; evaluate them and implement the most promising ones; confer with management when uncertain of a strategy's quality.
	Search the literature and the Internet for good ideas from noncompeting markets.

STRATEGY 2

Support (adapt with support; low rating + moderate fit), using coaching tactics	Enlist the aid of a co-worker or outsider with a reputation for creative marketing strategies in selecting a program. Further enlist this person's aid for the next several marketing campaigns.
	Build in specific performance measures to serve as both a reminder and an incentive.
	Place reminders, such as posters, around your work area, such as "If it is to be, it's up to me."

STRATEGY 3

Develop (low rating + good fit), using learning tactics	Identify a good training program that teaches creative marketing strategies.
	Subscribe to creative marketing and advertising magazines or websites for your industry.
	Allocate a healthy chunk of time for the next several campaigns until you get the hang of it and begin getting feedback that you like.
	Build in specific performance measures as both a reminder and an incentive.

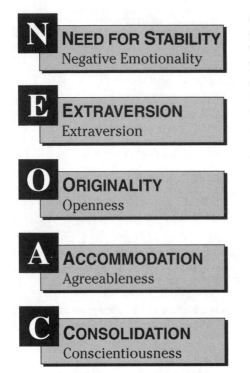

N NEED FOR STABILITY
Negative Emotionality

E EXTRAVERSION
Extraversion

O ORIGINALITY
Openness

A ACCOMMODATION
Agreeableness

C CONSOLIDATION
Conscientiousness

and then edited before being broadcast; this gave Jimmy a much less stressful production venue. A key factor in his realization of this was that he felt fine after producing the taped and edited program. This experience clarified his stress-filled discomfort with live telecasts, where little room for error exists. Ultimately, he decided to leave real-time sports and began producing television documentaries full-time. These productions were more forgiving and much less stressful to create, thereby accommodating his N+ score.

HRO Case Study 2
The Floundering Financial VP

Harry was a thirty-year-old MBA with six successful years of experience as a financial manager for a home builder when he accepted a position as the financial vice president for a commercial real estate developer. After three years on the job, his finance department of a dozen employees was in disarray, emotionally as well as professionally. After Harry had taken our battery of tests and we'd interviewed all of the relevant stakeholders associated with his success or failure, we uncovered three major discrepancies:

1. Harry was excessively submissive (A+) and was not sufficiently tough to challenge the strong egos of the developers. The result: he overpromised and avoided conflict.

2. He was spontaneous and undisciplined (C–), lacking the systematic, orderly approach so necessary to financial management. The result: deadlines were missed and budgets were overspent.

3. He demonstrated the capability for handling only a one-year time span of mental complexity, as described by Jaques's model (1994), about the time it takes to build a home and

turn it over to the new owner. (According to Jaques, people with a one-year time span for work can handle a task without supervision that takes no more than one year from beginning to end; given a task with a longer time span, they require more supervision and would flounder without it.) The time span of commercial development is about twenty-five years, involving acquisition and development of the land, construction, and long-term rental and management. The result: because the people who reported to him were more capable than he was, he couldn't give them the kind of help and resources they needed, and they didn't respect him.

The considered judgment of Harry's associates was that if a person was capable of learning commercial management, eighteen months should be adequate for the learning curve. The company decided to bring in a new financial vice president and offered Harry one of two ways to redesign the situation. He could either accept a lower-level job or look elsewhere for a less demanding position as a financial officer, with full outplacement assistance from the company. Harry chose to look elsewhere and is now comfortably and happily working in a less challenging job with another company.

In summary, we propose the following sequence for the HRO Model:

1. Define the performance competency.
2. Identify the ideal trait and talent infrastructure for the competency.
3. Assess the individual on the performance competency.
4. Assess the individual on the trait and talent infrastructure.
5. Identify any gaps between actual and ideal performance.
6. For each gap, assess the fit between the individual and the ideal infrastructure.
7. If the fit is close, develop or train the individual.
8. If the fit is poor, compensate or work around the gap with other strategies.

9. If the fit is somewhere in between, support or coach the individual in adapting to some situations with extra help and incentives.

Note: For further treatment of this subject, we highly recommend that you read *First, Break All the Rules* (Buckingham and Coffman, 1999). These two Gallup consultants report on their study of over eighty thousand managers in over four hundred companies. Their conclusions closely parallel our recommendations in this chapter. What we add to their ideas is the concept of trait infrastructure.

17

Learning Styles

Doing What Comes Naturally

The sculptor Michelangelo spoke of "discovering" the implicit shape contained within a block of marble, then chipping away until it was finally revealed. In much the same manner, the educator (trainer, teacher, coach) must discover the unique style of a learner in order to harness it to the desired knowledge. Learning is an active process in which learners must take information from the outside and make it a part of themselves, internalizing the information.

Each of us has our own unique style for learning. Learning styles are traits expressing themselves in a learning situation. Whether we're learning how to strengthen a skill or a body of knowledge (referred to in the business world as "development") or how to offset the effects of our limitations (known as "compensation"; see Chapter Sixteen for a discussion of the relationship between development and compensation), our appropriate learning style must be engaged in order to learn effectively.

Learning Style and the Big Five

Each of the Big Five personality dimensions has implications for how we learn best. The remainder of this chapter spells out the ways in which the natural behaviors associated with the three areas of each trait continuum (high and very high, midrange, low and very low) express themselves in learning situations. Whether you're a coach, a teacher, a trainer, a designer of learning materials and programs, or an individual learner who wants to be more effective, these strategies will be of interest to you. In order to form an IEP (Individual Educational Plan) for a specific individual, you'll need to know his or her Big Five scores. If they aren't available, you can estimate them by referring to the "clues" in Table 9.1, or by reviewing the range descriptions for the three ranges of the scales in Chapters Two through Six.

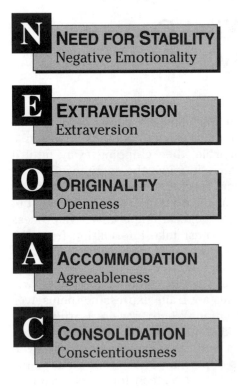

N NEED FOR STABILITY
Negative Emotionality

E EXTRAVERSION
Extraversion

O ORIGINALITY
Openness

A ACCOMMODATION
Agreeableness

C CONSOLIDATION
Conscientiousness

In addition to forming IEPs for individuals (including yourself!), you may also need to form GEPs, or Group Educational Plans. For example, say that you're preparing two training programs, one for a group of mechanical engineers and the other for a group of salespeople. Even if you don't have composite Big Five scores for the two groups, common sense (now that you've almost finished reading this book!) tells you that the first group will probably be more E– (solitary) and C– (spontaneous), while the second group will be more E+ (sociable) and C+ (ambitious). Thus, you would emphasize E– and C– strategies for the engineers and E+ and C+ strategies for the salespeople. For both groups, you would consider a balance of N– and N+, O– and O+, and A– and A+ strategies.

How N Affects Learning

Learners who are high or very high in N (N+ or N++, with scores over 55) would benefit from these learning strategies:

- Ensure that the learning environment is free of stress for the learners. If they're bothered by something, talk it through and get it out in the open and dealt with. A learner who has just left a stressful episode should be allowed to engage in something physical to relieve the symptoms, such as taking a ten-minute brisk walk, hitting a punching bag, shooting basketball, or pitching horseshoes.

- Consider using a journal, either verbal or visual, for learners to express what's bothering them, which can help them to get it off their minds.

- Typically, these learners appreciate having an instructional leader or facilitator.

- Be sure to process failure; for example, ask, "How will you approach this differently next time?" Minimize ways to fail so that they don't take it personally and become unmotivated.

- Protect the learners from potential sources of stress in the immediate environment, such as noise or an extremely hot or cold room.

The following strategies are for learners who score in the mid-range of N (N=, with scores between 45 and 55):

- Generally speaking, people who score in the middle range prefer a balance of learning strategies drawn from the two extremes—for example, not too much praise and encouragement (this can become tiresome) but not too little either (they need a certain amount of praise).

- On the other hand, some people in the middle range have a need for strategies of truly moderate intensity, rather than just a balance of the extremes. For example, rather than giving effusive and frequent praise or minimal, restrained praise, try giving recognition in a moderately inflected voice—that is, don't say either "That's fantastic!" or "Ho-hum, you've excelled again."

- Rather than being constantly available or, at the other extreme, simply there when they need you, try making "rounds" with them, just passing by from time to time and occasionally asking how things are going.

These strategies would be appropriate for learners who are low or very low in N (N– or N––, with scores below 45):

- As a general rule, these learners need a minimum of leadership. Be available to them, but let them work independently as much as possible.

- Speak calmly to them; they tend to be put off by emotional appeals, especially if they're also low in A.

How E Affects Learning

These strategies should be effective with learners who are high or very high in E (E+ or E++, with scores above 55):

- Employ learning activities that bombard the senses with colors, light, wind, smells, textures, tastes, and fragrances; emphasize physical activity. Think Disney!

- Employ physical rewards, such as food, picnics, or sports.

- Try to match their high energy in an authentic way—for example, by following their tempo of talking and walking.

- Provide opportunities for them to exercise leadership roles. Don't assume that they want or need privacy; being in the thick of activity is the norm for them.

- Have them engage in a dyad (a relationship between two people) as a helpful way to learn to be more comfortable with solitude.

- Assign or encourage tasks that are by nature active and social, such as discussing, demonstrating, interviewing, acting out, role playing, collaborating, leading, investigating, reporting, or working on a committee.

Consider these strategies for learners who are midrange in E (E=, with scores between 45 and 55):

- Generally speaking, those who score in the middle range prefer a balance of learning strategies drawn from the two extremes— for example, participation in loud, boisterous activity followed by quiet seatwork.

- On the other hand, some people in the middle range have a need for strategies of moderate intensity, rather than just a balance of the extremes. For example, instead of just balancing large-group activities with solitary ones, try using mostly small- to medium-sized group activities; instead of alternating between loud noise and quiet, employ a moderate rumble.

Try these strategies for learners who are low or very low in E (E– or E––, with scores below 45):

- More introverted learners can function well in groups, as long as two precautions are taken. First, allow them to prepare for group discussion by making notes, getting organized, developing a plan, preparing visuals or demonstrations, making a script, preparing a written agenda or plan ahead of time, and so forth. Second, limit their group discussion to a relatively small part of the day; it will drain their energy.

- Try to match their lower energy level by talking lower, talking or walking more slowly, and so on.

- Assign or encourage tasks that are calm and quiet by nature, such as reading, writing, drawing, organizing, keyboarding, collecting, sorting, or observing.

- Appeal to their uniqueness as a person.

How O Affects Learning

For learners who are high or very high in O (O+ or O++, with scores above 55), try these strategies:

- They have a twenty-four-hour-a-day curiosity, so feel free to use diverse examples to illustrate a concept; for instance, you can use a technical example even if the person isn't technically proficient.

- Don't expect these learners to continue with a particular kind of activity for too long: they like variety.

- Verbally recognize them when they persist in a particular activity for an extended period; they may become uncomfortable staying with a single experience for a long time, but their long-term success will depend on their being able to defer the need for variety on occasions when they need to deal with monotonous and repetitious details.

- Remember that their interests may be chaotic and lack integration, coordination, and a clear sense of priorities.

- Take the opportunity to help them to establish priorities and get organized, or encourage them to take time out to do it for themselves.

- In a team context, have them perform roles such as designer, creative writer, brainstormer, interviewer, or interpreter. Appeal to their interest in theory and aesthetics.

Following are considerations for learners who are midrange in O (O=, with scores between 45 and 55):

- Generally speaking, people who score in the middle range prefer a balance of learning strategies drawn from the two extremes—for example, some exploration of new and different topics balanced with practice and development of expertise in the more familiar ones.

- On the other hand, some people in the middle range have a need for strategies of truly moderate intensity, rather than just a balance of the extremes. When introducing unfamiliar concepts or subjects to these people, emphasize familiar elements so that they can build on their identification with these elements. When planning a learning episode, provide just enough structure to help them get started: too much may bore them by failing to involve their imagination in the planning process, while too little may frustrate them because of their need for a minimum level of guidance or structure.

These strategies should be effective for learners who are low or very low in O (O– or O––, with scores below 45):

- Because people who are low in O have a narrower range of interests, build on their existing interests; for example, use baseball or cooking examples to explain mathematical concepts.

- They don't possess a strong curiosity, especially about unfamiliar subjects, so present them with questions and options rather than expecting them to come up with their own.

- Introduce learnings in small steps, linking each step to the next before putting a whole model together.

- In a team context, encourage them to perform in such roles as counter, assembler, data analyst, builder, copier, technical writer, describer, or observer. Appeal to their typical interest in financial and economic values.

How A Affects Learning

These strategies should be effective for learners who are high or very high in A (A+ or A++, with scores above 55):

- Remember that they have very little appetite for competition and prefer cooperative methods.

- In a disagreement or argument, they tend to submit, defer, or otherwise give in to the desires of others; pair them with a midrange scorer who can serve as a negotiator.

- These people tend to be more trusting than most; encourage them to develop a healthy skepticism, ask questions, and look out for their own needs in other ways.

Following are considerations for learners who are midrange in A (A=, with scores between 45 and 55):

- Generally speaking, people scoring in the middle range prefer a balance of learning strategies drawn from the two extremes—for example, taking part in some activities that are highly competitive but also some that demand cooperation.

- On the other hand, some people in the middle range have a need for strategies of truly moderate intensity, rather than just a balance of the extremes. Build on their natural inclination to favor win-win situations by using them as negotiators and facilitators; they do less well when they are either arguing a singular point of view or passively observing the debate. These people also tend to be genuinely androgynous and don't identify with solely feminine and nurturing or masculine and aggressive roles; don't use them in either a "bad-guy" role (class monitor, time-keeper, sergeant-at-arms) or a "teacher's pet" role (don't point them out as the best example or spend excessive time in dialogue with them).

These strategies should be effective for learners who are low or very low in A (A– or A––, with scores below 45):

- They have a heavy appetite for competition and a strong need to win and enjoy debates, simulations, and other activities in which there are clear winners. Their ability to cooperate will increase if you precede the activity with aerobic exercise.

- They identify with traditionally "masculine" values, behaviors, and attitudes, such as aggressiveness, competition, dominance, and hierarchy. Attempt to involve them in learning strategies that build positively on these values, such as debates, competitive simulation games, and evaluative activities.

- In an argument or disagreement, they tend to dominate or beat the other person down; pair them with midrange scorers who will serve as a buffer, or negotiator, between them and others.

How C Affects Learning

These strategies should be effective with learners who are high or very high in C (C+ or C++, with scores above 55):

- They are motivated by traditional indicators of achievement: rankings, awards, status symbols or titles, high grades or scores, breaking records, winning elections.

- They prefer to set one or more goals and pursue them without being distracted by unrelated activities. Assist them in establishing appropriate goals; otherwise they may ferociously pursue goals that are nonproductive.

- They can delay their need for rewards or recognition until completion of the work; resist the temptation to specify rewards or incentives in advance that might stifle their imagination.

- They naturally prefer and work well with structure, rules, and guidelines. They should be encouraged to resist their need to structure things when it would be premature and just explore the situation instead.

Following are considerations for learners who are midrange in C (C=, with scores between 45 and 55):

- Generally speaking, people who score in the middle range prefer a balance of learning strategies drawn from the two extremes—for example, taking part in highly structured and focused activities as well as unstructured, spontaneous ones.

- On the other hand, some people in the middle range have a need for strategies of truly moderate intensity, rather than just a balance of the extremes. For example, rather than providing a complete plan or structure or none at all, try providing the bare outlines of a plan and letting them fill in the details. Or rather than focusing on only one activity for long stretches or on pure spontaneity, try working for a moderate amount of time on one activity, then switching to a second activity, alternating between the two.

These strategies should be effective for learners who are low or very low in C (C– or C––, with scores below 45):

- These people typically resist activities that require them to proceed from beginning to end without interruption; they are "parallel processors" who enjoy being involved in several processes simultaneously.

- Because they typically are not organized, provide suggestions, crutches, or other specific ways to help them organize their learning activities and work space. Pair them with a C+ in order to facilitate organization. Recognize their small victories.

In summary, working with learning styles involves nothing more than building on the learners' natural behaviors and values in order to help them acquire new information, skills, and concepts. Excessive reliance on their weaker behaviors is stressful, and stress interferes with learning. As far as the two of us are concerned, of the two opposite behaviors, practice and creation, we're weaker in practice, stronger in creation. Asking us to spend much time in practice is stressful; we're more motivated and more effective in a role in which we are more creative. We're writers, not "poofreaders"!

Part
Four

Personal

Applications

Your Own Big Five

18

The Big Five After Five

Family, Friends, Romance, Health, Hobbies, and Spirituality

Until now, we've spent most of this book primarily relating the Big Five to the workplace. "But," you ask, "what about when the workday ends? Is the Big Five still relevant?" Our answer: absolutely!

Frequently, when we conduct workshops, people ask if we can give the Big Five to a significant person in their personal lives. We refer these inquirers to our global consulting network. Our website, http://www.centacs.com, lists these certified Big Five consultants by geographic region. Although we specialize in workplace applications of the Big Five, we think it's vitally important for people to understand the other individuals in their lives: partners, family, friends, and even enemies. This book won't enable you to measure your scores or those of the other people in your life, but it should help you to

My life's amusements have been just the same Before and after standing armies came.

—Alexander Pope

anticipate probable profiles. Knowing them, you may use Chapter Eleven on relationships, Chapter Nine on influence, or Chapter Twelve on teams to think through your partner, your volunteer group, your walking buddy, your hobby friends, or your family unit. If you find communication or conflict difficulties, try using some of the suggested strategies to improve the relationship or at least make it more tolerable.

We have summarized here some of the more significant and practical applications from personality research in various areas. As a way of pointing out the relationship of these "after-five" profiles to the rest of this book, as well as justifying their inclusion, let us suggest that the information in this chapter could provide an excellent basis for marketing and advertising decisions. For example, if you want to sell phone cards to people who are prone to homesickness, you would want the content of your advertising to reflect the unique traits associated with homesickness in the third paragraph below. (All facet references below are to the NEO PI-R model.)

Family

Academic performance: C and O appear to have a particular influence on the way a student approaches school. Students who are O+C− tend to emphasize extracurricular pursuits, while those who are O−C+ tend to become subject experts, winning prizes such as the "Math Cup." Students who are O− and C− tend to just get by, satisfying the minimum requirements, while those who are O+C+ tend to take the all-around academic honors, such as Phi Beta Kappa and Dean's List. Students who are O=C= tend to be well-rounded, doing well enough in both academics and extracurricular activities.

Aging: Activity (NEO E4) and ambition (NEO C4) tend to decrease in the elderly, but only moderately. All the other facets appear to remain stable.

Homesickness: Children and adults who get homesick tend to have the following profile: N+E−O−A+C1−.

Insomnia: People who are N+O+A+ are prone to have it.

Mate preferences: Research suggests that, all other things being equal, the most socially desirable, or ideal, mate tends to be N–E+O+A+C+. People who are O+A+C+ tend to select mates who match their O+A+C+. People who are N–O+A+ tend to report the greatest mate satisfaction, while those with the opposite profile (N+O–A–) tend to report more dissatisfaction with their mates, regardless of the mate's profile.

Motivation: People who are N+E– generally tend to be motivated by fear of punishment ("Be bad and you'll be given a time-out"), while those who are N–E+ tend to be more motivated by the promise of rewards ("Be good and we'll go shopping").

"Zapper" behavior: People who are A–C– tend to use the TV remote control primarily for control of others, while N+ zappers tend to use it for content avoidance.

Friends

We may choose our friends for different reasons. Sometimes we want someone similar to us, and sometimes we want someone different to stimulate us.

Getting to know you: People who, according to the NEO model, are N5++ (low urge control), E34– (low assertiveness and low activity), O2– (low aesthetics), A4+ (deferring), and C–– need to know someone a long time before calling that person a friend.

Sympathy: People who are most likely to show sympathy to others tend to be N–E+A+.

Use of "B.S.": People who often engage in "B.S." (extemporizing without foundation!) tend to have this profile on the NEO model: A–A13–A2++C––C2–C1345––.

NEO PI-R Facets	
N1	Worry
N2	Anger
N3	Discouragement
N4	Self-consciousness
N5	Impulsiveness
N6	Vulnerability
E1	Warmth
E2	Gregariousness
E3	Assertiveness
E4	Activity
E5	Excitement seeking
E6	Positive emotions
O1	Fantasy
O2	Aesthetics
O3	Feelings
O4	Actions
O5	Ideas
O6	Values
A1	Trust
A2	Straightforwardness
A3	Altruism
A4	Compliance
A5	Modesty
A6	Tender-mindedness
C1	Competence
C2	Order
C3	Dutifulness
C4	Achievement striving
C5	Self-discipline
C6	Deliberation

Romance

When we want romance, do we want long-term stability with a partner over time or a mad, passionate fling with someone who is completely unlike us and with whom we don't see ourselves growing and maturing? As a general rule, opposites attract for the short term but people with similar profiles tend to be more satisfied with one another for the long term, as discussed in Chapter Eleven. When people who are different on one or more traits are together for a lifetime, it's imperative that they accept these differences and not take them personally. For example, an E+ shouldn't accuse an E– spouse of not wanting them to go out together; the E– doesn't want to go out period, regardless of the partner. Here are some other interesting findings:

Crying: People who are N+E+A+C– have a tendency to cry and/or get teary-eyed.

Delay of gratification: People who are O+A+C+ tend to have a greater capacity to delay gratification.

Love styles: Research has identified six distinct styles of expressing love: Ludus (game playing) tends to be associated with N+E+O+C– profiles; Storge (friendship or parental) is associated with N–C1– profiles; Pragma (logical, practical) doesn't appear to be associated with any particular profile; Mania (possessive, dependent) is associated with N+E+O+C– profiles; Eros (erotic) is associated with N–C1+ profiles; and Agape (all-giving and selfless) is associated with the C1– profile.

Health

Much information is emerging on how closely physical health is aligned with personality and mental health (see Howard, 2000c). Several major studies are under way that examine these trends; one of the most notable is currently being conducted by the Medical School at the University of North Carolina at Chapel Hill, where the general health of alumni who have taken the Big Five is being tracked and studied over time. Other studies have resulted in these findings:

Alcohol: People who are prone to consume somewhat more alcohol than usual tend to be N+, and especially N1+.

Exercise: The people who are the most consistent in adhering to their workout schedule tend to be N–-E+O–C++. Moderate workout patterns are especially seen among people who are O++C+, while strenuous workout patterns are more common among those who are N–E++O–C++.

Healthiest profile: The healthiest profile tends to be N–E+O–A+C+.

Longevity: People who are A2–A5+C5+ tend to live the longest.

Motives for working out: Stress reduction tends to be the reason that people who are E+O++ work out, while people who are just E+ have more "social" reasons. Both N++ and E+ people tend to work out to improve their appearance and/or weight, while N–, E++, and O+ profiles do it primarily for enjoyment. Overall health and wellness is the primary motive for E+A+C+ profiles.

Perceived obstacles to getting exercise: Lack of time is the typical excuse for N+ and O+; lack of energy for N+, E–, and C–; lack of motivation for N+ and C–; and embarrassment for N++ and C–.

Risk behavior: People with O+ profiles are prone to take risks with substances; those with N+A–C– profiles take risks in traffic. People with N–E+A+C+ profiles tend to be the most successful in avoiding accidents. Wellness behaviors in general tend to be most embraced by those who are N–E+A+C+. People who are A–C– tend to get the most traffic tickets from moving violations.

Runners: Long-distance runners tend to be E+.

Vegetarians: People who claim to be vegetarians tend to have a profile of E14+O+O3+A3+.

Hobbies and Interests

How do you define a hobby? One of the areas we described earlier is the O scale on the Big Five. We know that the higher the score, the more interests an individual is likely to have, although not all of them are hobbies. Still, here is some emerging research on hobbies and interests, much of which *Cent*ACS has collected.

Artistic talents: People who have multiple artistic talents tend to be N5+O++C1245–. Those who see themselves as actors tend to be O++1++234+A3–5––C––125––4–; as composers, N+3++N5+E–– 234–O++123+C14–; as dancers, O+; as dramatists, A2+C–2–5––; as illustrators, O+O2+A2–; as journalists, E4+O++3++A3+; as painters, O++C5–; as poets, O++A3++C5–; as pop musicians, O1+C4–; as singers, N3–O+; as writers, O++A3++; and as writers of fiction, O+A3+C5–.

Ballet: People who are interested in ballet tend to be O+C–.

Crafts: People who are interested in crafts tend to be E+O+O1+C5–.

Culinary arts: People who are interested in culinary arts tend to be N4–E3+O++A5–.

Fashion: Those who follow and/or buy current fashion in clothing or accessories tend to be N++1245+E+2++A–A2–.

Languages: N+E+ profiles tend to learn to speak a foreign language most easily, while N+E– profiles tend to learn to write one most easily.

Lotteries: Participation in lotteries tends to be more common among people who are O–.

Music: People who prefer loud bass volume typically are E+C–. Those who play brass instruments tend to be N1–E+; guitar or banjo, N5+O1+A2++C1–; keyboard or piano, N–E1+O+A–; percussion instruments, A5––; string instruments, O+; and woodwind instruments, N1+E1–A3–4+. Vocalists tend to be N1+O+A1–.

Personal grooming: Those who pay the most careful attention to clothing, dressing, and personal grooming tend to be N+4++ E14+O3+A–5–C++235+.

Reading interests: Arts and crafts are associated with N–A–C–; entertainment with N+E+C–; fiction with O+C–; fitness and health with E+O–; mechanical subjects with O–A–; psychology and philosophy with N–A+; religion and scripture with N–O–A+; science and math concepts with N–A–; and wildlife, hunting, and fishing with E+O–A–.

Shopping: Those who shop in order to browse without necessarily buying tend to be N+5++E3–C3–.

Sports: Those who are A–– tend to have the greatest air of self-confidence. E–A–– profiles tend to believe in their own abilities. E– people are more likely to dedicate themselves to improvement. A+ profiles are the most adaptable to new suggestions. Those who play for the team, not the self, tend to be A++, and those with the most positive attitude in practice tend to be O–A++. A++ people are the most supportive of their teammates and the most willing to listen to criticism. A+ profiles are the most willing to sacrifice other things for the sport. And E– people work hardest to improve their weaknesses.

Sports profile: From a coach's point of view, the ideal overall sports profile is E–O–A+.

TV programs watched: Hobby shows tend to be watched by those who are A2–; news shows by N4–5––E34+O3+A–4–5––C++13++45+; sports shows by E14++O–C5++; popular movies by N+13+5++ E3––4–C–13––; soap operas by N5++E34––O––2––A5+C––13––; documentaries by O++12++C+1++3+; popular music and dance shows by N5++E34––O2––A1––A3–C––13––4–; sitcoms by N15+ 4++E3–O–O2–A3––; science fiction by O++O2+; crime, mystery, and spy shows by E++E3++; adventure and thriller shows by E+A–4––C–; cartoons and children's programs by E4––A–C–1––; classic theater, drama, or art cinema by E1+O++12++; and lighter, contemporary drama by E1+O+1+A+34+.

TV watching: Those who are N+23++45+E1–O––3–A––23–4–– tend to watch the most hours of television on a weekly basis.

Volunteering: O+ and A+ tend to be the most willing to release test results, while E+, O+, and A+ tend to be the most willing to participate in a longitudinal study.

Spirituality

Many people take their spirituality very seriously and wonder about those who don't, worrying about them and prodding them to believe. Some individuals consider spirituality to be a very personal matter that they don't discuss openly. Others display a spiritual facade in the interest of being able to do business or relate to someone in a particular religious community. Interestingly, some clear research patterns have emerged:

Attendance: People with the most regular attendance at religious services tend to be N–A+.

Denomination: Those who belong to liberal congregations tend to be O+, and those who belong to fundamentalist congregations tend to be O–.

Motives for participation: Researchers have identified three primary motives for participating in religious activities: extrinsic, intrinsic, and questing. Extrinsic motives are utilitarian; for example, people may believe that church, temple, or mosque attendance will be good for business or a convenient method of moral education for their children. Extrinsically motivated people tend to be E+. Intrinsic motives are pious and altruistic; these people tend to be A++C+. The questing motive is common among those who are O+C+ and is characterized by a genuine interest in finding ever more meaningful answers to some of life's basic questions about where we stand in the scheme of things.

Miscellaneous

Education: People with the most years of education tend to be O+.

Profanity: People who are A–C– tend to use more profanity.

Sense of humor: People who are E–O3– tend to appreciate jokes involving incongruity resolution, while jokes involving nonsense appeal more to those who are E+O3+. Sexual jokes are more appreciated by those who are N+E+O3+A3–.

Although interesting, these various research areas still leave us wanting to know more about ourselves and others. In our estimation, because of the strong interest in the Five-Factor Model of personality in the research community worldwide, a large, growing body of information about the Big Five will become relevant to all aspects of our lives. We look forward to exploring it with you in future editions of this book!

19

At the End of the Day

Accepting Who You Are, but Not Bowing to Fate

Finally, now that we have discussed personality in all its multiple permutations, the question arises: what if you don't like your personality? What if this current person is not who you want to be from now on? After all is said and done, can you change?

There are three possible answers: yes, no, and maybe. Some solid research exists suggesting that people who are naturally high in C (remember that unrelenting goal orientation) can make conscious changes and stick to them, especially if those changes propel them toward their chosen goal. These people seem to have more success when they work with some type of job coach, career counselor, or work mentor. They may also come closer to achieving their change goals when they undergo

Our ship would come in much sooner if we'd only swim out to meet it.

—E. C. McKenzie,
Fourteen Thousand
Quips and Quotes

traditional therapeutic counseling. For the rest of us who are midrange or low in C, changing who we are for the long term is more difficult. However, this is not to say that we can't do something outside our natural comfort zone if we are determined enough.

When I (Jane) decided to obtain a master's degree in business administration in the mid-1980s, I gave it considerable thought because I wanted the credentials for the kind of consulting work that Pierce and I were doing. Going back to school as a thirty-three-year-old graduate student wasn't as easy for me as school had been when I was an undergraduate at age eighteen with a part-time secretarial job. In addition to studying and homework, I now had a family, career, and community life to think about.

Knowing my need for variety and a rapid pace and having a less than high C score on the Big Five, I ultimately decided to enter a well-respected two-year executive MBA program at Wake Forest University, two hours away from my home. Even though I was offered a scholarship to go through a local traditional evening program, taking one course a semester for six years while keeping my eye on the long-term goal seemed too long. Instead, twenty-two months after entering the program, I had a degree in hand. If I'd taken the longer, more traditional route, I'm not sure that I'd have been able to stick with the degree goal over six years. The very nature of the shorter program disallowed the tendency for procrastination that C= and C– people experience: I took twelve course hours every semester, with a full thesis written over the summer after the first year and a set time for faculty consultation, an unchanging cohort of classmates to exert peer pressure, and so on. (Research shows that a C– can achieve best when the job is well-defined and provides a greater degree of structure.)

One other deciding personality factor for me was my N– score. Fortunately, I can handle stress, and in the two years between 1985 and 1987, the MBA program certainly produced volumes of stress. Prime examples included

- Don, the infamous professor who wrote each student's name on a playing card and then shuffled the deck before calling the name on the top card

- Volumes of case studies to read and research papers to write

- Team study group dynamics between smokers and nonsmokers

- A three-hour mountain hike, with no trail, at the outset of the program when the MBA program dropped us off at Outward Bound for five days to foster teamwork

If I had been N+ instead of N– when I started graduate school, I might have been unable to finish the program because of personal guilt at occasionally passing on shopping with my teenage daughter or being far away while one of my older sisters handled most of my mother's cancer surgery and recovery during the two years I was in the program. Someone scoring N+ would probably achieve better in a longer-term program where a semester can be missed and made up later to take time out for pressing work or family issues.

If you want to push yourself outside your personality comfort zone, you have to know yourself and what you may potentially be facing. Once you have digested the contents of this book or attended a Big Five training session, you should be able to understand how successful or unsuccessful you might be. You also have to realize the potential health risks people set themselves (or others) up for over time when they try to change from being a square peg to becoming a round peg in order to fit into a round hole in the workplace.

As we thoroughly discussed in Chapter Fourteen, the nature-nurture issue is not a myth, nor is it something we can easily dismiss in either ourselves or others. Swimming against the current of our personality infrastructure as we try to compensate, support, or develop a competency or fit a preestablished job description is not easily accomplished. Although we might be able to make some headway, the channel crossing will be much easier for people who are swimming with the current of their personality rather than battling to swim upstream against their nature.

In business terminology, the bottom line is that we may be able to temporarily shift our personality or take on a job that's unnatural for us for the good of the team, the partnership, or the company. But for the long haul, our organization and our personal health will be much better served by placing ourselves and others in jobs that "fit" our personalities rather than by "force-fitting" them.

The workplace needs Human Resource Optimizers—those of us who will optimize our own work and that of others regardless of our titles or assigned responsibilities. The Big Five model is the vocabulary, the tool, the method to help us understand our individual differences and optimize the contributions we and others can make.

At the end of the working day, we will only find satisfaction when our jobs fit us well. That essence of satisfaction and sense of belonging are what most of us crave from our daily work. In some small measure, we hope that this book has helped you to find, think about, and create ideas, plans, procedures, techniques, or career goals that will enable you to achieve both belonging and, ultimately, genuine comfort and satisfaction with your personality and your work.

Appendix

Time Line Illustrating the History of the Development of the Big Five

1936
Allport and Odbert (1936) challenge the personality psychology research community to find the smallest possible number of synonym clusters in the approximately 4,500 personality-descriptive words from the unabridged English dictionary.

1946
Cattell (1946) proposes his solution to Allport and Odbert's challenge: the 16-PF, with its sixteen synonym clusters.

1949
Donald Fiske (1949) proposes a five-factor solution, with some differences from the "correct" solution.

1961
Ernest Tupes and Raymond Christal (1961), U.S. Air Force personnel researchers with access to mainframe computers, arrive at the five-factor solution to Allport and Odbert's challenge. This solution is essentially the same as the one we know today as the Big Five, or the Five-Factor Model.

1963
Warren Norman (1963) of the University of Michigan confirms the Tupes and Christal solution.

1960–1980
Personality psychology is in virtual exile: the behaviorists reign, with their assumption that personality traits don't exist. Instead, they hold that all behavior is learned and situational, without consistency from situation to situation (cf. Mischel, 1968).

1980 The Western Psychological Association meets in Honolulu. A panel of personality researchers declares that the Big Five—N, E, O, A, and C—successfully solves Allport and Odbert's 1936 challenge.

1981 IBM introduces the PC (personal computer).

1984 The SPSS (Statistical Package for the Social Sciences) offers factor analysis software for the IBM PC. For the first time, the average personality researcher with a personal desktop computer can perform factor analysis without having to stand in line to use a mainframe computer.

Mid-1980s With PCs and factor analysis software now available, scholarly articles that confirm the validity of the Five-Factor Model begin to appear in the literature.

1985 Paul Costa and Robert McCrae, once holdouts against the Big Five, decide to add A and C to their 1976 NEO test (Costa and McCrae, 1985); their test soon becomes the standard for measuring the Five-Factor Model (Costa and McCrae, 1992). Their norms are based on their work with the Baltimore Longitudinal Study of Aging, the longest and largest ongoing study of normal adult personality development over the life span.

1993 Pierce and Jane Howard offer the first Big Five certification training program through *Cent*ACS, the Center for Applied Cognitive Studies, in Charlotte, North Carolina.

1995 The Howards publish the first human resources trade literature article related to the Five-Factor Model, "Buddy, Can You Paradigm?" in *Training and Development.*

2000 The Howards introduce the WorkPlace Big Five ProFile for assessing the Big Five in work settings.

Bibliography

Allport, G. W. (1937). *Personality: A Psychological Interpretation.* Austin, TX: Holt, Rinehart and Winston.

Allport, G. W., and Odbert, H. S. (1936). "Trait Names: A Psycho-lexical Study." *Psychological Monographs, 47*(211).

Anderson, K. J. (1994, June). "Impulsivity, Caffeine, and Task Difficulty: A Within-Subjects Test of the Yerkes-Dodson Law." *Personality and Individual Differences, 16*(6), 813–829.

Avia, M. D., and others (1995, July). "The Five-Factor Model: II. Relations of the NEO-PI with Other Personality Variables." *Personality and Individual Differences, 19*(1), 81–97.

Azar, B. (1995, July). "Predicting Workers' Success Overseas." *APA Monitor, 26*(7), 32.

Baldwin, T. T., and Ford, K. (1988). "Transfer of Training: A Review and Directions for Future Research." *Personnel Psychology, 41,* 63–105.

Barrick, M. R., and Mount, M. K. (1991). "The Big Five Personality Dimensions and Job Performance: A Meta-Analysis." *Personnel Psychology, 44,* 1–26.

Barrick, M. R., and Mount, M. K. (1993). "Autonomy as a Moderator of the Relationship Between the Big Five Personality Dimensions and Job Performance." *Journal of Applied Psychology, 78*(1), 111–118.

Ben-Zur, H., and Wardi, N. (1994, September). "Type A Behavior Patterns and Decision Making Strategies." *Personality and Individual Differences, 17*(3), 323–334.

Bigazzi, J. M., Kello, J. E., and Marciano, P. L. (1999). "The Relationship Between NEO Personality Inventory and Job Performance as Moderated by Job Autonomy." Unpublished paper presented at January 23 CentACS Big Five Conference, Charlotte, NC.

Blue, L. (1999). "The Relationship Between Personality Traits and Influence Strategies: A Comparison of College Business Students and Business Professionals." Unpublished doctoral dissertation, The Union Institute Graduate School, Cincinnati, Ohio.

Booth-Kewley, S., and Vickers, R. R., Jr. (1994). "Associations Between Major Domains of Personality and Health Behavior." *Journal of Personality, 62*(3), 281–298.

Brandstaetter, H. (1994, June). "Pleasure of Leisure—Pleasure of Work: Personality Makes the Difference." *Personality and Individual Differences, 16*(6), 931–946.

Buckingham, M., and Coffman, C. (1999). *First, Break All the Rules.* New York: Simon & Schuster.

Burgoon, J. K., Stern, L. A., and Dillman, L. (1995). *Interpersonal Adaptation: Dyadic Interactions Patterns.* New York: Cambridge University Press.

Cattell, R. B. (1946). *The Description and Measurement of Personality.* Yonkers, NY: World Book.

Cialdini, R. B., Trost, M. R., and Newsom, J. T. (1995). "Preference for Consistency: The Development of a Valid Measure and the Discovery of Surprising Behavioral Implications." *Journal of Personality and Social Psychology, 69*(2), 318–328.

Cochran, K. B. (1998). *The Relationship Between Explanatory Style and the Big Five Theory of Personality.* (Master's thesis, University of North Carolina at Charlotte). (Research Report No. BFR-5). Charlotte, NC: Center for Applied Cognitive Studies.

Costa, P. T., Jr., and McCrae, R. R. (1985). *The NEO Personality Inventory Manual.* Odessa, FL: Psychological Assessment Resources.

Costa, P. T., Jr., and McCrae, R. R. (1992). *NEO PI-R: Professional Manual.* Odessa, FL: Psychological Assessment Resources.

Crant, J. M. (1995). "The Proactive Personality Scale and Objective Job Performance Among Real Estate Agents." *Journal of Applied Psychology, 80*(4), 532–537.

Csikszentmihalyi, M. (1990). *Flow: The Psychology of Optimal Experience.* New York: HarperCollins.

Csikszentmihalyi, M. (1996). *Creativity: Flow and the Psychology of Discovery and Invention.* New York: HarperCollins.

Davies, R. (1970). *Fifth Business.* New York: Viking Penguin.

DeFruyt, F., and Mervielde, I. (1997, July). "The Five-Factor Model of Personality and Holland's RIASEC Interest Types." *Personality and Individual Differences, 23*(1), 87–103.

Detterman, D. K., and Sternberg, R. J. (1993). *Transfer on Trial: Intelligence, Cognition, and Instruction.* Norwood, NJ: Ablex.

Digman, J. M., and Inouye, J. (1986). "Further Specification of the Five Robust Factors of Personality." *Journal of Personality and Social Psychology, 50,* 116–123.

Fiske, D. W. (1949). "Consistency of the Factorial Structures of Personality Ratings from Different Sources." *Journal of Abnormal Social Psychology, 44,* 329–344.

Forabosco, G., and Ruch, W. (1994, April). "Sensation Seeking, Social Attitudes and Humor Appreciation in Italy." *Personality and Individual Differences, 16*(4), 515–528.

Fournies, F. F. (1999). *Coaching for Improved Work Performance* (rev. ed.). New York: McGraw-Hill.

Furnham, A., Crump, J., and Whelan, J. (1997). "Validating the NEO Personality Inventory Using Assessors' Ratings." *Personality and Individual Differences, 22*(5), 669–675.

Gaines, S. O., Jr., and Reed, E. S. (1995, February). "Prejudice: From Allport to DuBois." *American Psychologist, 50*(2), 96–103.

Gardner, H. (1983). *Frames of Mind: The Theory of Multiple Intelligences.* New York: Basic Books.

Gould, S. J. (1993). *Eight Little Piggies: Reflections in Natural History.* New York: Norton.

Hayes, T. L., Roehm, H. A., and Castellano, J. P. (1994). "Personality Correlates of Success in Total Quality Manufacturing." *Journal of Business and Psychology, 8*(4), 397–411.

Hersey, P., and Blanchard, K. (1988). *Management of Organizational Behavior* (5th ed.). Englewood Cliffs, NJ: Prentice Hall.

Hogan, R., Curphy, G. J., and Hogan, J. (1994). "What We Know About Leadership: Effectiveness and Personality." *American Psychologist, 49*(6), 493–504.

Holland, J. L. (1996). "Exploring Careers with a Typology: What We Have Learned and Some New Directions." *American Psychologist, 51*(4), 397–406.

Horner, K. (1996). "Locus of Control, Neuroticism, and Stressors: Combined Influences on Reported Physical Illness." *Personality and Individual Differences, 21*(2), 195–204.

Howard, J. M., and Howard, P. J. (1998). *Team Building and the Big Five: A Trainer Manual for Use with the Big Five Workbook.* Charlotte, NC: Center for Applied Cognitive Studies.

Howard, P. J. (2000a). *69 Words.* (*Cent*ACS Research Report No. 3). Charlotte, NC: Center for Applied Cognitive Studies.

Howard, P. J. (2000b). *40 Words.* (*Cent*ACS Research Report No. 4). Charlotte, NC: Center for Applied Cognitive Studies.

Howard, P. J. (2000c). *The Owner's Manual for the Brain: Everyday Applications from Mind-Brain Research* (2nd ed.). Austin, TX: Bard Press.

Howard, P. J. (n.d.). Files on record for miscellaneous validity studies conducted from 1990 to present (information is proprietary to corporate clients). Charlotte, NC: Center for Applied Cognitive Studies.

Howard, P. J., and Howard, J. M. (1993). *The Big Five Workbook: A Roadmap for Individual and Team Interpretation of Scores on the Five-Factor Model of Personality.* Austin, TX: Leornian Press.

Howard, P. J., and Howard, J. M. (1995, September). "Buddy, Can You Paradigm?" *Training and Development, 49*(9), 28–34.

Howard, P. J., and Howard, J. M. (1997). *Rapport and Influence Strategies: A Planning Workbook for Enhancing Your Rapport and Influence with Significant Others in Your Personal and Professional Life.* Charlotte, NC: Center for Applied Cognitive Studies.

Howard, P. J., and Howard, J. M. (2000). *User's Manual for the WorkPlace Big Five ProFile.* Charlotte, NC: Center for Applied Cognitive Studies.

Howard, P. J., Howard, J. M., and Medina, P. L. (1996). "The Big Five Locator: A Quick Assessment Tool for Consultants and Trainers." *The 1996 Annual.* San Diego: Pfeiffer.

Jaques, E. (1994). *Human Capability.* Falls Church, VA: Cason Hall.

Johnson, J. A., and Ostendorf, F. (1993). "Clarification of the Five-Factor Model with the Abridged Big Five Dimensional Circumplex." *Journal of Personality and Social Psychology, 65*(3), 563–576.

Kelley, H. H. (1979). *Personal Relationships.* Hillsdale, NJ: Erlbaum.

Kelley, H. H., and Thibaut, J. W. (1978). *Interpersonal Relations: A Theory of Interdependence.* New York: Wiley.

Kiesler, D. J. (1996). *Contemporary Interpersonal Theory and Research: Personality, Psychopathology, and Psychotherapy.* New York: Wiley.

King, L. A. (1995, May). "Personal Strivings and the Five-Factor Model." Paper presented at the Midwestern Psychological Association, Chicago.

Kyl-Heku, L. M., and Buss, D. M. (1996, October). "Tactics as Units of Analysis in Personality Psychology: An Illustration Using Tactics of Hierarchy Negotiation." *Personality and Individual Differences, 21*(4), 497–517.

Leslie, J. B., and Fleenor, J. W. (1998). *Feedback to Managers: A Review and Comparison of Multi-Rater Instruments for Management Development.* Greensboro, NC: Center for Creative Leadership.

Lombardo, M. M., and Eichinger, R. W. (1996). *The Career Architect Development Planner.* Minneapolis, MN: Lominger Limited.

Lombardo, M. M., and Eichinger, R. W. (1998). *For Your Improvement* (2nd ed.). Minneapolis, MN: Lominger Limited.

Mager, R., and Pipe, P. (1997). *Analyzing Performance Problems, or "You Really Oughta Wanna"* (3rd rev. ed.). Atlanta: Center for Effective Performance.

McCrae, R. R., and Costa, P. T. (1989). "Reinterpreting the Myers-Briggs Type Indicator from the Perspective of the Five-Factor Model of Personality." *Journal of Personality, 57*(1), 17–40.

McCrae, R. R., and Costa, P. T. (1990). *Personality in Adulthood.* New York: Guilford Press.

McDaniel, R. N. (1992). "The Relationship Between Personality and Perceived Success of Organizational Change" (Doctoral dissertation, The Fielding Institute). *Dissertation Abstracts International,* 53/06-B, p. 3196.

Mischel, W. (1968). *Personality and Assessment.* New York: Wiley.

Morr, S., and Howard, P. J. (1999). "The Big Five at Work." Unpublished manuscript available from the Center for Applied Studies, Charlotte, NC.

Morr, S., and Howard, P. J. (2000). "The Big Five at Play." Unpublished data available from the Center for Applied Studies, Charlotte, NC.

Norman, W. T. (1963). "Toward an Adequate Taxonomy of Personality Attributes: Replicated Factor Structure in Peer Nomination Personality Ratings." *Journal of Abnormal and Social Psychology, 66,* 574–583.

Ones, D. S., Viswesvaran, C., and Schmidt, F. L. (1995, June). "Integrity Tests: Overlooked Facts, Resolved Issues, and Remaining Questions." *American Psychologist, 50*(6), 456–457.

Ornstein, R. (1993). *The Roots of the Self: Unraveling the Mystery of Who We Are.* San Francisco: Harper San Francisco.

Piedmont, R. L., and Weinstein, H. P. (1994). "Predicting Supervisor Ratings of Job Performance Using the NEO Personality Inventory." *Journal of Personality, 128*(3), 255–265.

Robinson, D. G., and Robinson, J. C. (1995). *Performance Consulting: Moving Beyond Training.* San Francisco: Berrett-Koehler.

Rose, R. G. (1993). *Practical Issues in Employment Testing.* Odessa, FL.: Psychological Assessment Resources.

Saucier, G., and Goldberg, L. R. (1998, August). "What Is Beyond the Big Five?" *Journal of Personality, 66*(4), 495–524.

Schein, E. H. (1993). *Career Anchors: Discovering Your Real Values* (rev. ed.). San Diego, CA: Pfeiffer.

Sternberg, R. J. (1988). *The Triarchic Mind: A New Theory of Human Intelligence.* New York: Viking Penguin.

Tokar, D. M., and Swanson, J. L. (1995). "Evaluation of the Correspondence Between Holland's Vocational Personality Typology and the Five-Factor Model of Personality." *Journal of Vocational Behavior, 46,* 89–108.

Tornow, W. W., London, M., and CCL Associates. (1998). *Maximizing the Value of 360-Degree Feedback: A Process for Successful Individual and Organizational Development.* San Francisco: Jossey-Bass.

Tuckman, B. W. (1965). "Development Sequence in Small Groups." *Psychological Bulletin, 63*(6), 384–399.

Tupes, E. C., and Christal, R. E. (1961, May). *Recurrent Personality Factors Based on Trait Ratings.* (Aeronautical Systems Division Report ASD-TR-61-97). Lackland Air Force Base, TX: Aeronautical Systems Division, Personnel Laboratory.

U.S. Department of Labor, Employment, and Training Administration. (1991). *Dictionary of Occupational Titles* (4th ed.). Lincolnwood, IL: VGM Career Horizons.

Wang, M. (1997). *Personality Traits and Athletic Behaviors: An Examination of Personality in College Aged Athletes and Their Sport Behaviors.* (Senior thesis, Davidson College, Davidson, NC). (*Cent*ACS Research Report No. 1). Charlotte, NC: Center for Applied Cognitive Studies.

Watson, J. B. (1925). *Behaviorism.* New York: Norton.

Wilson, E. O. (1975). *Sociobiology: The New Synthesis.* Cambridge, MA: Harvard University Press.

Yik, M.S.M., and Tang, C. S. (1996). "Linking Personality and Values." *Personality and Individual Differences, 21*(5), 767–774.

Index

About
*Cent*ACS

The vision of *Cent*ACS, the Center for Applied Cognitive Studies, is to optimize people through a global professional network. The company is the primary location of Pierce and Jane Howard's work and research with the Big Five. It is an information-based e-commerce company, developing and publishing materials, training and certifying consultants to use the Big Five, and conducting research to support the Five-Factor Model of personality and other brain-related research designed to help people work more effectively.

Established in Charlotte, North Carolina, in July 1986 by Jane Mitchell Howard, M.B.A., managing director, and Pierce J. Howard, Ph.D., director of research, the company is currently located in a 5,900-square-foot facility with offices and a learning center only a mile from downtown Charlotte. At this writing, *Cent*ACS has six full-time employees, five part-time employees, and a growing network of over one thousand certified and qualified Big Five consultants around the world, trained by the Howards and other *Cent*ACS Master Trainers.

The mission of *Cent*ACS is to establish personality assessment and brain research standards for the twenty-first century by building a global network of internal and external consultants and international affiliate companies who use the Five-Factor Model of personality, the Human Resource Optimizer Model, and related brain research in their work. Through certification and advanced training programs, learning conferences, valid and respected test instruments, on-line e-services, a scoring services bureau, and other resources, *Cent*ACS provides cutting-edge information, high-quality products, and support services.

Primarily, the company operates within the United States with certified consultants located from California to Massachusetts, from Florida to Wisconsin. Many Fortune 500 companies, medium-to-small companies, university MBA programs, and consulting companies are customers of *Cent*ACS. Outside the United States, *Cent*ACS is currently affiliated with four companies that work with the Big Five in their respective geographic areas.

For further information about how you may use the Big Five in your organization or in your work, or to contact *Cent*ACS or its affiliate companies, please refer to the following information:

United States and all other countries not listed below:

*Cent*ACS, the Center for Applied Cognitive Studies
1100 Harding Place, Charlotte, NC 28204-2825
Contact: Josephine Washington, Sales Consultant Director
Telephone: +1.704.331.0926
Toll Free: +1.800.BIG.5555
Fax: +1.704.331.9408
E-mail: info@centacs.com
Website: http://www.centacs.com
WorkPlace Big Five ProFile on-line: http://www.centacs.com
NEO PI-R on-line: http://www.centacs.com
On-line store: http://www.centacs.com
On-line certification programs: http://www.centacs.com
On-line qualifications: http://www.centacs.com

Mexico: People Value una División de e-Siglo

Contact: Malú Velázquez
Telephone: +525.536.1555, ext. 162
E-mail: mvelazquez@e-siglo.com
Website: http://www.e-siglo.com

Singapore, Indonesia, and Malaysia: Research Communication, Ltd.

Contact: Dr. Shirley Lim
Telephone: +65.332.0855
E-mail: rescomm@singnet.com.sg
Website: http://www.researchcommunication.com

Holland, Germany, France, Spain, and Japan: PiMedia

Contact: Martijn van der Woude
Telephone: +31(0)346.55.90.10
E-mail: mvdwoude@pimedia.nl
Website: http://www.pimedia.com

**United Kingdom and the Republic of Ireland:
Resourcing Excellence, a PACT Group Company**

Contact: Bridget Seddon
Telphone: +44.(0)1963.250885
E-mail: bridget@pact-group.com
Website: http://www.pact-group.com

TO ORDER ADDITIONAL COPIES OF

The Owner's Manual for Personality at Work
How the Big Five Personality Traits Affect Performance,
Communication, Teamwork, Leadership, and Sales

Paperback $19.95

VISIT YOUR FAVORITE BOOKSTORE
OR CALL TOLL FREE

1-800-945-3132

OR FAX YOUR ORDER TO 512-282-5055

VISA / MASTERCARD / DISCOVER / AMERICAN EXPRESS ACCEPTED

QUANTITY DISCOUNTS ARE AVAILABLE
CONTACT

AN IMPRINT OF LONGSTREET PRESS
2140 Newmarket Parkway, Suite 122
Marietta, GA 30067
770-980-1488 phone   770-859-9894 fax
www.bardpress.com

How to Use and Complete Your Big Five Profile Estimate

WHILE YOU ARE READING THIS BOOK

As you read Chapters Two through Six, follow the instructions in each chapter's text for marking your likely score directly on the foldout page. Using the descriptions in the chapter, decide where you think you would score for each of the five scales. With a pen or pencil, make a mark on the Big Five Profile Estimate to indicate your probable score (unless you're reading this as a library book or a borrowed book). You may find it helpful to leave the foldout page open beside the book's text; it can serve as a quick reference guide as you read about the scales and their workplace applications.

AFTER YOU HAVE FINISHED READING THIS BOOK

If you didn't estimate your Big Five scores while you read Chapters Two through Six, take a moment now to estimate your scores. In order to assist you, we have included some brief descriptions of the low, middle, and high regions of each personality trait scale next to the foldout page. Read the three paragraphs that describe each scale. Based upon our explanation of a continuum, decide into which range your personality falls. If you're uncertain about where you score, return to the appropriate chapter for additional information.

IF YOU ALREADY KNOW YOUR ACTUAL SCORES ON THE WORKPLACE BIG FIVE PROFILE OR THE NEO PI-R

You may have attended a training program, a team-building retreat, or a coaching session on the Big Five where a consultant gave you a printed report of your scores on the Big Five. If so, simply mark your scores in pen or pencil directly on the foldout; you may then read the book with the foldout open to directly reference your own scores.

OTHER USES

Once you have estimated your own scores, you may find yourself trying to estimate the scores of one of your team members or a colleague. This is a very appropriate use of the Big Five Profile Estimate. Our only caution would be to remind you that you may not know quite as much about your team member or colleague as you think you do. Still, your estimate can help you to create strategies that will work more effectively or communicate more clearly with that individual. See Table 9.1 for help with projecting another person's profile based on observable behaviors.

FURTHER HELP

If you need assistance in locating consultants who can lead you, your team, your department, or your organization through a complete program where you can receive your actual Big Five scores and personal feedback about them, please visit the *Cent*ACS website at http://www.centacs.com.